LEGENDS OF WARFARE
NAVAL

USS Iowa (BB-61)

The Story of "The Big Stick" from 1940 to the Present

DAVID DOYLE

Schiffer Publishing Ltd

4880 Lower Valley Road • Atglen, PA 19310

Designed by Justin Watkinson
Type set in Impact/Minion Pro/Univers LT Std

All photos are from the collections of the US National Archives and Records Administration unless otherwise noted.

ISBN: 978-0-7643-5417-5
Printed in China

Published by Schiffer Publishing, Ltd.
4880 Lower Valley Road
Atglen, PA 19310
Phone: (610) 593-1777; Fax: (610) 593-2002
E-mail: Info@schifferbooks.com
www.schifferbooks.com

For our complete selection of fine books on this and related subjects, please visit our website at www.schifferbooks.com. You may also write for a free catalog.

Schiffer Publishing's titles are available at special discounts for bulk purchases for sales promotions or premiums. Special editions, including personalized covers, corporate imprints, and excerpts, can be created in large quantities for special needs. For more information, contact the publisher.

We are always looking for people to write books on new and related subjects. If you have an idea for a book, please contact us at proposals@schifferbooks.com.

Acknowledgments

This book would not have been possible without the gracious help of many individuals and institutions. Beyond the invaluable help provided by Dave Way and the staff of the Pacific Battleship Center, as well as the staff of the National Archives, I am indebted to Tom Kailbourn, Scott Taylor, Dana Bell, Tracy White, Rick Davis, Dave Baker, Roger Torgeson, Sean Hert, Chris Hughes, and James Noblin. Their generous and skillful assistance adds immensely to the quality of this volume. In addition to such wonderful friends and colleagues, the Lord has blessed me a wonderful wife, Denise, who has tirelessly scanned thousands of photos and documents for this and numerous other books. Beyond that, she has an ongoing source of support and inspiration.

All contemporary photos by author unless otherwise noted.

Contents

Foreword

David Doyle, author of more than 100 books on various military subjects, has assembled the most comprehensive, illustrated history of one of America's greatest warships, battleship USS *Iowa* BB-61. His historical narrative covers *Iowa*'s design in 1938, her construction and launch, all three commissioning periods and war time service, and through to her restoration as a current museum memorial warship. There have been a number of books written that document the rich history and technical characteristics of the four *Iowa* class battleships. This book, however, using mostly previously unpublished photographs—including rare color examples from World War II—provides the reader with an exciting read and a fresh visual journey of battleship *Iowa*'s rich history.

Built in 1940, battleship *Iowa* was in service for almost twenty years and in the reserve fleet for another fifty years. She was designated the "Worlds' Greatest Ship" when launched in 1942. *Iowa* was awarded nine battle stars for her service during World War II, and two additional battle stars for Korean War service. First commissioned in 1943, she stood the *Tirpitz* watch before hosting President Roosevelt on his journey to the Tehran Conference of that year. Transitioning to the Pacific in 1944, she continued her war duties while escorting the fast attack aircraft carrier task forces in their journey across the South Pacific, and completed the war in Tokyo Bay during surrender activities in September 1945.

Activated for a second commissioning in 1951 for the Korean War, *Iowa* fired twice as many 16-inch and 5-inch projectiles during that conflict than she fired during World War II, and was awarded two more battle stars. Her big guns, heavy armor, and great speed ensured her relevance for a third commissioning during the Cold War, when she was refurbished and upgraded with the latest technology and weapons in 1983. The fourteen award ribbons and eleven battle stars are still proudly displayed on her bridge wings, paying tribute to her seventy years of service.

Iowa was the last battleship in the world to be saved from the scrapyard when she was awarded to the non-profit Pacific Battleship Center (PBC) in September 2011. Of the forty-nine battleships commissioned for the American Navy, eight have survived as memorial museum warships on display in the United States. With a three million dollar grant from the state of Iowa, PBC's staff, along with the aid of hundreds of volunteers, refurbished and repainted *Iowa* at the Port of Richmond, California, in 2012. Towed to the Port of Los Angeles in May 2012, *Iowa* opened to the public on July 7, 2012, as the only memorial museum battleship on America's continental west coast.

The Southern California waterfront has a long history with the American battleship. On August 9, 1919, the Pacific Battle Fleet steamed into San Pedro Bay (today part of the Ports of Los Angeles and Long Beach, California) and for the next twenty years, San Pedro Bay was considered the battleship home port for the US Pacific Fleet. Often referred to as "Battleship Country," an observer of the time might find as many as fifteen battleships anchored in San Pedro Bay. Nearby Long Beach Naval Station was *Iowa*'s home port during her first two commissionings, so how very appropriate it is that *Iowa*'s final berth would be back in Battleship Country.

I am delighted to see such an excellent history of *Iowa* finally being published, and highly recommend it to warship historians and model builders, *Iowa*'s very own Veterans, and *Iowa*'s museum visitors.

David Way, Curator
Battleship *Iowa*, May 2017

Introduction

Born out of the limitations of the London Naval Treaty, the USS *Iowa* would be the lead ship of the final class of battleship built by the United States, and the last class of battleship to be operated by any navy.

Following World War I, a series of international treaties had been put in place limiting the number, size, and armament of warships to be operated by the signatories, which included most of the world's powers. These early attempts at arms limitation treaties were moderately successful, with the naval architects of most signatories soon stretching the limit of the terms. In 1934, Japan gave formal notice that it was withdrawing from the treaties. Germany, by the way, was not involved in the naval treaties as the Treaty of Versailles, which marked its capitulation in World War I, already placed significant prohibitions on Germany's armaments.

By March 1936, only the United States, Great Britain, and France were bound by any of the treaties. In March 1938, in view of ship building activities worldwide, these nations invoked an escalator clause in the Second London Naval Treaty, which raised the maximum capital ship displacement allowed from 35,000 tons to 45,000 tons.

Warship design has always been a battle of desires vs. practicality. Bigger guns increase displacement, as does heavier and/or more extensive armor protection. More speed requires larger machinery, which requires a larger hull to house it, and of course the machinery has to be protected by armor, which increases the weight. In order to maintain a given speed, more power is required, and the cycle starts again.

Under the initial clauses of the treaties, battleships were limited to 35,000 tons displacement, and the *North Carolina* and *South Dakota* classes adhered to that. Armed with nine 16-inch, 45-caliber guns, the six ships of these two classes had top speeds of about twenty-six knots.

As early as 1923, the United States had considered the possibility that it would need to defend the Pacific against Japan. At such extreme distances from the US, the fleet would be extremely vulnerable to cruiser and aircraft carrier attacks, and many felt that fast, powerful battleships would be required to counter this threat.

In January 1938, Capt. A.J. Chantry, head of the Design Division of the Bureau of Construction and Repair, instituted a study of designs of 16-inch gun ships that could be accommodated by the 110-foot wide locks of the Panama Canal, that were capable of making thirty-five knots.

As these studies and requirements were refined, the form of the American "fast battleship" came together, and on June 2, 1938, a proposal for a 33-knot, 9-gun, 44,559-ton vessel was presented to the Navy General Board. By Act of Congress on May 17, 1938, construction of two ships of the new design was authorized. Contracts for construction of two ships built to the new design were signed on July 1, 1939. The first ship of the new class, BB-61, would be the *Iowa*, with BB-62 being named *New Jersey*.

CHAPTER 1
Construction

Because the commercial shipyards that were experienced in modern battleship construction, Newport News Shipbuilding and Drydock Company, New York Shipbuiding, and Bethlehem Steel's Fore River shipyard in Quincy, Massachusetts, were already tied up building the earlier *South Dakota* class battleships, the contract to build *Iowa* was issued to the New York Navy Yard.

There was an issue, however. The General Board had asked that the main battery turrets for the ships be made to accommodate the 16-inch, 50-caliber (heavy naval gun calibers are the length of the barrel divided by the bore) Mark II gun. An abundant supply of these guns were available, as they had been produced for the CC-1 battlecruiser and BB-49 battleship classes, but the ships themselves were cancelled in 1922 when the initial treaty was adopted, leaving the Navy with a large inventory of the guns. The Bureau of Ordnance obligingly sketched a lightweight turret, with a new slide, requiring a barbette of 37 feet, 3 inches. The Bureau also developed detailed drawings of an alternate turret, this a scaled-up version of the turrets on *North Carolina* and *South Dakota*, and requiring a 39-foot diameter barbette.

In order to get the maximum speed out of the new hull and provide an acceptable level of protection, the Bureau of Construction and Repair elected to go with the 37-foot, 3-inch turret design. Unfortunately, the Bureau of Ordnance produced detailed plans for the larger turret. Thus, for a five-month period the two agencies worked on parallel, but different paths. In early November 1938, the turret drawings were delivered, and the discrepancies in diameter caused considerable upheaval, leading to a special meeting of the General Board.

By this point in time of course, Congress had been sold on the characteristics of the ship as the Bureau of Construction and Repair had presented, which included the more powerful 16-inch, 50-caliber gun, precluding the possibility of building a less capable vessel.

The Bureau of Ordnance responded rapidly to this debacle, engineering a new 16-inch, 50-caliber gun and turret that would fit the vessel design. While meaning that the surplus Mark II guns could not be used, the use of the new Mark VII 16-inch, 50-caliber guns and associated turrets, approved by the Secretary of the Navy on December 10, 1938, allowed the construction of the vessels to proceed.

Similarly, the New York Navy Yard proposed an improved machinery layout, with an alternating fire room, engine room arrangement, with two boilers in each fire room, and each propeller shaft having its own engine room. Such an arrangement would reduce the size, and thus the vulnerability, of each machinery space, as compared to the BuC&R initial plans. Despite the modest delay as well as increased cost the Yard design would entail, the benefits were such that the Bureau approved the changes and the plans were modified accordingly.

The keel of *Iowa* was laid on June 27, 1940, with RADM C.H. Woodward, chief of the Bureau of Construction and Repair, driving the first rivet. For two years the massive steel form of *Iowa*'s hull rose above the builder's ways in New York. With Mrs. Henry Wallace smashing a bottle of champagne on her bow, the sleek hull was launched on August 27, 1942.

The keel-laying ceremony marks the official beginning of construction of a ship. The battleship *Iowa*'s was on June 27, 1940, at the Navy Yard, New York, also known as the Brooklyn Navy Yard. Rear Admiral Clark H. Woodward, chief of the Bureau of Construction and Repair, US Navy, is seen here with another admiral as they drive the first rivet into the keel of the *Iowa*.

On September 30, 1940, two months after the keel-laying, the progress of work on the hull of the *Iowa* is seen from amidships off the starboard beam facing aft. The frames, or lateral ribs of the ship, are under construction in the hold. The frames were numbered consecutively from the bow to the stern beginning with one, and they received watertight plating on the bottom, in between them, and on the top, forming three layers of skin down the hull bottom for extra protection against torpedoes. This feature is called a triple hull. Some parts of the hull toward the bow and the stern were of double-hull construction. In the area in the foreground, the lower compartments of the triple hull will contain fresh water and feed water, while the upper compartments will be voids. In the background are neat stacks of hundreds of frame sections, which will be installed one by one.

On the same day and from the same vantage point as the preceding photo, the hull of the *Iowa* is viewed facing forward, showing the assembly of the intricate components that made up the frame. Along the right side of the photo, the starboard side of the shell, the outer layer of the hull plating, is taking shape. The frame on the bottom of the hull will be built outward to connect to the shell.

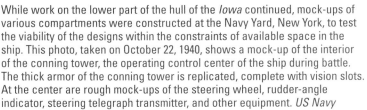

While work on the lower part of the hull of the *Iowa* continued, mock-ups of various compartments were constructed at the Navy Yard, New York, to test the viability of the designs within the constraints of available space in the ship. This photo, taken on October 22, 1940, shows a mock-up of the interior of the conning tower, the operating control center of the ship during battle. The thick armor of the conning tower is replicated, complete with vision slots. At the center are rough mock-ups of the steering wheel, rudder-angle indicator, steering telegraph transmitter, and other equipment. *US Navy*

A mock-up for the ammunition-handling room for twin 5-inch/.38-caliber dual-purpose gun mount number 2 is depicted. Toward the top are representations of the powder hoists; near the bottom is the location of the gun-firing storage-battery box. In the right background is a mock-up of the layout for storage space for eighty rounds of 5-inch ammunition. Mock-ups of control boxes are to the right. *US Navy*

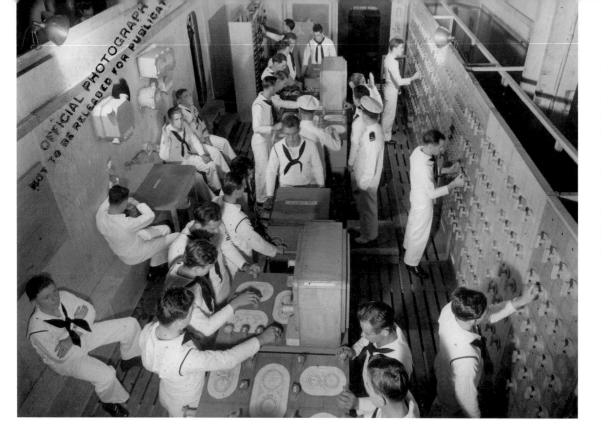

Another October 22, 1940, photograph shows a mock-up for the after secondary battery plotting room. This compartment of the *Iowa* would contain equipment for coordinating and controlling the 5-inch/.38-caliber gun mounts. In the center of the compartment are mockups of two Mk.1 computers and two stable elements, a device that corrects for the tilting of the ship. To the right is the fire-control switchboard, for controlling the flow of signals and data through the secondary battery's fire-control system.

This is a mock-up of the after main-battery plotting room, for controlling and coordinating the 16-inch/50-caliber guns. In the foreground are the plotter's table and the battle-telephone switchboard. To the left is the fire-control switchboard. The mock-up enabled designers to analyze and fine-tune the ability of crewmen to execute their duties within the given space.

In a December 30, 1940, view from above midships facing aft, watertight transverse bulkheads separating machinery spaces are in place. In the extreme foreground is the rear of fire room number 1. The first bulkhead, number 93 (also coinciding with the frame of that number), and the next one, number 103, would enclose engine room number 1. Farther aft are lateral bulkheads for alternating fire rooms and engine rooms. Each fire room housed two boilers, for a total of eight boilers, while each engine room contained one propulsion unit, for a total of four.

The hull of the *Iowa* is viewed from above facing forward. In the foreground is transverse bulkhead 111. The farthest bulkhead is number 87, to the immediate front of which will be the forward emergency diesel generator and distilling plant. To the sides of the bulkheads, the shell of the hull continues under construction. Alongside the hull is scaffolding for the workers.

Behind the nearest bulkhead, number 127, in this April 1, 1941, photo of the *Iowa* facing aft is Fire Room Number 3. The upper parts of boilers number 6, left, and 5, right, are visible in this compartment, surrounded by scaffolding. The next compartment is Engine Room Number 2. In the background, the bow is still in a very early stage of construction.

In a June 27, 1941, midship view of *Iowa* facing aft, the upper parts of all eight boilers are visible, two abreast; they are partially obscured by protective material positioned tent-style over the boilers. The horizontal cylinders at the tops of the boilers are the steam drums. Issuing from the top of each steam drum is an elbow-shaped steam outlet. Generator tubes and superheater tubes are routed up to the drums. The boxy structures under covers on the inboard sides of the steam drums house the economizer elements. Between the successive fire rooms, the tops of the engine rooms are in the process of being plated over to create the third deck.

The stools, or foundations, of the two forward 16-inch/50-caliber gun turrets, Turrets 1 and 2, are under construction in the background in this October 3, 1941, photograph, taken above amidships facing forward. The stools were stationary parts of the turret, supporting the revolving gun house and 16-inch guns, and containing operating machinery for the turret and storage space and hoisting equipment for ammunition. Around these stools will be built the tube-shape, heavily armored enclosure called the barbette, extending from the armored decks, below decks, up to the weather decks.

In a companion view to the preceding one, the hull of the *Iowa* is viewed from above facing aft on October 3, 1941. In the foreground is the stool of Turret 2. Aft of it is transverse bulkhead 87, which formed the front end of Fire Room Number 1. Framing with large lightening holes is being assembled from the top of bulkhead 87 aft. This will support the second deck, the main armored deck, extending from aft of Barbette 2 to the front of Barbette 3. Below this framework was the splinter deck, which was not a usable deck because of its proximity to the armored deck.

In the interval between the preceding October 1941 photos and this one taken on December 31, 1941, America had entered World War II, and winter had set in. The view is from amidships looking forward. Portable conical roofs had been installed over the turret stools to keep out snow. Arrayed on the second deck are construction materials, welding equipment, webs of electrical wires, and mechanical components to be installed in the ship. To the sides of the hull are the torpedo bulkheads that will form part of the protection system. On the outboard side of the third bulkhead is the armored belt. Whereas on many warships the armored belt was on the exterior of the hull, on the *Iowa*-class battleships the belt was an internal one, 12.1 inches thick at the top, tapering to 1.62 inches at the bottom, and extending from the second deck down to the top of the triple bottom.

Taken on the same date as the preceding view, this photo is facing aft from amidships, with the temporarily covered stool of Turret 2 in the foreground and the stool of Turret 3 in the background. To the port side of the stool of Turret 2 toward the lower right of the photo is some of the framing, with large, round lightening holes, for the armored second deck. On the underside of the framing can be seen part of the splinter deck, designed to protect the crew and equipment from splinters should a bomb detonate on the armored deck immediately above.

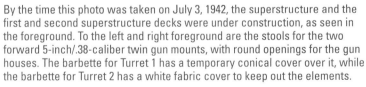

By the time this photo was taken on July 3, 1942, the superstructure and the first and second superstructure decks were under construction, as seen in the foreground. To the left and right foreground are the stools for the two forward 5-inch/.38-caliber twin gun mounts, with round openings for the gun houses. The barbette for Turret 1 has a temporary conical cover over it, while the barbette for Turret 2 has a white fabric cover to keep out the elements.

The progress of construction on the *Iowa* is documented in this July 3, 1942, photo facing aft from amidships. In the foreground to the rear of the first two lateral bulkheads, the space in the center of the superstructure with the wooden ladder in it is the forward uptake; the aft uptake is farther to the rear. Through these uptakes, exhaust gases from the boilers are routed up to the smokestacks. In the background, the portable, conical cover for the barbette of Turret 3 has been removed from the barbette and is on the starboard side of the quarterdeck.

On August 26, 1942, one day before her launching, the battleship *Iowa* is viewed off her port bow. The hull has a coat of paint, and the boot topping along the waterline has been applied, a black plastic substance that masks the oil and sludge that tends to cling to ships in harbors. Suspended from a cable along the bow is an anchor chain. To the rear of the bow, workmen are making adjustments to the poppets: frames that support the bow before and during launching. The poppets are attached to the hull with a series of cables.

Another August 26, 1942, photograph shows the *Iowa*'s stern on the building ways, as viewed from the port side. Wooden shoring and steel poppets are installed to support selected parts of the hull. The two port propeller shafts and their struts are visible, as is the mounting for the port rudder, in line with and aft of the port inboard propeller shaft. On each side of the stern are tubs for quad 40 mm antiaircraft gun mounts.

The lower part of the port side of the hull near the stern of *Iowa* is shown on the day before launching, with a closer view of the two port propeller shafts and the stern poppet installed between the shafts. The outboard propeller shafts were supported by shafts, while the two inboard shafts were routed through skegs incorporated into the bottom of the hull. The propellers will be mounted on the shafts after launching while the ship is in dry dock.

The starboard side of the stern area of the *Iowa* is shown in an August 26, 1942, photograph. The horizontal wooden boards attached to the rear of the stern poppet, situated at right angles to the longitudinal centerline of the hull, are called the mask: a structure designed to slow down the momentum of the ship as it glided out on the water upon launching.

CHAPTER 2
Launching and Fitting-Out

Spurred by the nation's new war footing, *Iowa* was ready for launch seven months ahead of schedule. However, those same wartime exigencies meant that the launching ceremony itself lacked some of the pomp that previously had accorded the launch of a new capital ship. The massive warship, the largest battleship then launched by the United States, was christened by vice president and Iowa native Henry A. Wallace's wife, Ilo Browne Wallace, along with their daughter, Miss Jean Wallace, serving as maid of honor. First Lady Eleanor Roosevelt was in attendance. The First Lady wrote in her journal:

> "Yesterday morning, Miss Thompson and I, with Capt. John McCrae, the president's naval aide, breakfasted early and went over to the Brooklyn Navy Yard to witness the launching of the biggest battleship that the United States has ever built. Battleships of this size must slide down the ways at exactly the right minute, and at 10:36 a.m. exactly, the battleship began to move, and Mrs. Henry Wallace, wife of the vice-president, broke the bottle of champagne on her bow and christened her '*Iowa*'."

It is a wonderful sight to see a big ship take to the water for the first time, particularly in the yard where the men who have built her are standing around with pride shining in their eyes as they see their handiwork completed and a prayer in their hearts for the ship's good fortune at sea.

Yesterday it seemed to me to have an added significance, for all about us were men in uniform in far greater numbers than usual. One could not help thinking of how many boys that ship will hold when it finally sails off to take its place in the great world battle now going on. We know that all branches of the services are equally important, and that they depend on each other and must function as a group to be really successful. A strong Navy is important, but without strong air protection, battleships are far more vulnerable than they were before the advent of the airplane."

The launching of a warship, while a significant event, by no means indicates that the ship is complete. Months of work lay ahead for the shipyard workers constructing *Iowa*. First at a fitting out pier in the New York Navy Yard, and then at a basin at the then-new New York Navy Yard Bayonne Annex, craftsman installed weapons, wiring, teak decking, bunks, and mess equipment, and a myriad of other items large and small.

The battleship *Iowa* presents her sleek bow to the camera on the date of her launching, August 27, 1942. The wooden scaffolding that had encased the hull during construction had been cleared away, and the ship was being readied for sending her sliding down the ways. Because of the exigencies of wartime, the budget for the launching ceremony was much smaller than had been the custom in the pre-war years, and by special order of the Naval authorities, the number of attendees was to be limited. Suspended from each side of the bow are bundles of anchor chains, which will slow the progress of the ship after entering the water.

The christening party and the spectators at the *Iowa*'s launching are seen from the battleship's forecastle on August 27, 1942. Marked in white on the bow are draft numbers, signifying the amount of draft of the ship. The ship's waterline as designed is marked as a white line along the black boot topping. *Pacific Battleship Center*

The aft part of the *Iowa* has entered the water during her launching on August 27, 1942. The ways had been heavily greased to reduce the massive amount of friction generated by the movement of the hull. Several persons are standing on a temporary bridge erected above the main deck amidships.

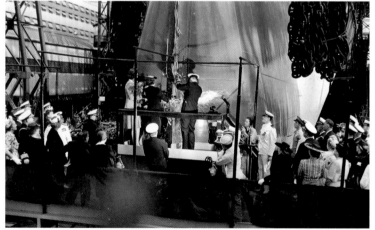

The sponsor of the *Iowa,* Mrs. Ilo Browne Wallace (left), the wife of the vice president of the United States, Henry Wallace, and her party, including her maid of honor, her daughter, Miss Jean Wallace (back to the camera), pose on the christening platform moments before the launching.

Mrs. Henry Wallace has just smashed the ceremonial bottle of champagne on the bow of the *Iowa* in the christening ceremony. A moment after this photo was taken, the ship was released from its remaining tethers and it began its slide down the ways.

Dressed out fore to aft in flags and pennants, the *Iowa* is about to be towed by a fleet of tugs to her fitting-out dock at the Navy Yard, New York, where the ship will be completed over the coming months. The first two levels of the superstructure have been enclosed, rising above which are the two smokestacks and the tower for the aft main-battery director.

The *Iowa* is viewed from another perspective after her launching on August 27, 1942. Portable conical covers are visible above the barbettes of Turret 1 and Turret 3. A large, temporary shelter is on the main deck aft of Turret 3.

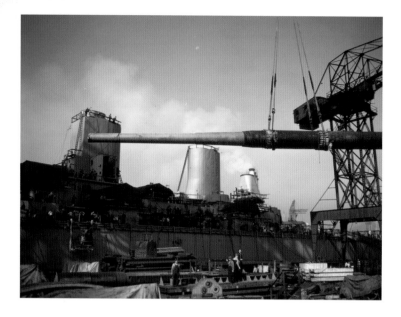

In the early weeks after her August 27, 1942, launching, the *Iowa* received her 16-inch/50-caliber Mk.7 guns: a total of nine, distributed to three turrets. Here, a 16-inch gun barrel is being lowered to the fitting-out dock, where it and other barrels will be kept until they are to be mounted on the ship.

Workers at the fitting-out dock are rubbing down the 16-inch/50-caliber gun barrels soon to be mounted in the *Iowa*'s turrets. Some of the workmen are rubbing their hands over the surface to detect any imperfections or damage to the barrels.

In this photo, some of these guns are on the fitting-out dock at the Navy Yard, New York, being prepared for mounting in the turrets. In the interim since the preceding photo was taken, a tub for a Mk.51 director had been installed on the forward port corner of the tower for the aft main-battery director. The director this tub would later hold was for remotely controlling a quad 40 mm antiaircraft gun mount.

On the same occasion as the preceding photo, likely in the fall of 1942, workers at the Navy Yard, New York, inspect 16-inch/50-caliber gun barrels for imperfections. The 16-inch/.50-caliber Mk.7 guns were of a built-up design, created heating a jacket, hoops, and locking and yoke rings and sliding these expanded components over the tube. The assembly was then cooled and shrunk, forming a unified barrel, and then a liner was inserted and rifled.

In a view from the foredeck of the *Iowa*, the right 16-inch/50-caliber gun has been mounted in *Iowa*'s Turret Number 1. The armored enclosure of the turret, the gun house, is only partially assembled, consisting at this point of side plates of .75-inch STS (special treatment steel). Later, the armor of the gun house will be built up, employing different thicknesses of Class A and Class B armor over STS plates. To the rear of Turret 1 is Turret 2, under construction, with no guns mounted yet. In the background with a ladder leaning against it is the front of the forward smokestack. In the right distance is one of the Navy Yard's massive hammerhead cranes.

This original color photograph showing the installation of the right 16-inch/50-caliber gun in Turret 1 is a companion piece to the preceding photo, having evidently been taken on the same date. A workman in denim bib overalls and a white shirt is standing on the collar of the upper shield of the gun. Behind the shield may be seen the left counter-recoil cylinder of the gun. In the far-left background are the Navy Yards' building ways, where the hull of the *Iowa* had been constructed.

In the interval after the preceding photos were taken, work had begun on the forward fire-control tower of the *Iowa*, as viewed from the starboard front corner of the first level of the superstructure. Eventually, the forward main-battery director would be mounted on top of this tower, and the foremast would be attached to the rear of it. The tower adjoined the front of the forward smokestack. These combined structures and the aft smokestack, the top of which is visible here, were painted in a yellowish finish, likely zinc chromate primer. Temporary scaffolding is arranged around the tower.

On the same date as in the preceding photograph, work proceeds on Turret Number 2. All three 16-inch/50-caliber guns are mounted, and the .75-inch-thick STS inner plates are present on the sides of the gun house. To the far left, a truck-mounted portable crane has been brought into play on the main deck.

In a view apparently taken on the same date as the preceding two photos, Turrets 1 and 2 and the forward fire-control tower are viewed from the foredeck. Turret 1 is traversed to port, and all three 16-inch/50-caliber guns are mounted in that turret. Large plugs called tompions are visible in the muzzles of the guns of Turret 2; the tompions kept foreign objects out of the bores of the barrels.

Turret Number 3 of the *Iowa* is viewed from above during the ship's fitting-out period at the Navy Yard, New York. The 16-inch gun barrels have a whitish-rust coloration on them. Note the zinc chromate primer on the armor plates of the splinter shield in the foreground and the spot welds on the vertical braces on the left side of the shield. Networks of electrical lines are strung over metal stands on the deck below, and temporary sheds made of corrugated galvanized steel are on the deck.

In October 1942, the *Iowa* traveled down the East River and through New York Harbor to the recently opened Naval Supply Depot of the Bayonne Annex, Navy Yard, New York, for completion work in Dry Dock Number 1. Here the battleship passes under the Brooklyn Bridge en route to Bayonne. There was only five feet of clearance for the battleship under the Brooklyn Bridge at low tide. The vantage point is on the main deck to the starboard of the aft fire-control tower. The gun houses of the 5-inch/.38-caliber twin gun mounts are covered with tarpaulins, the gun barrels sticking out from under them.

Tugboats are maneuvering the *Iowa* toward Dry Dock Number 1 at the Naval Supply Depot at Bayonne on October 20, 1942. Shipyard workers and a few Naval officers are on the deck of the ship. In the foreground is a temporary shelter over the still roofless Turret Number 2, the guns of which are trained obliquely to starboard.

The *Iowa* enters the dry dock at Bayonne on October 20, 1942. Scaffolding encases the forward fire-control tower. A good view is available of the unfinished left side of the gun house of Turret Number 2, with openings cut in it for the rangefinder and the sight-setter's telescopes. What appears to be a temporary bridge is to the lower front of the forward fire-control tower. In the background is the Structural and Machine Shop of the Bayonne Annex.

This photo and the following two form a series taken on January 15, 1943, to document the progress of construction on the battleship *Iowa*. By now, the 5-inch/.38-caliber twin gun mounts are in place; and platforms are installed on the smokestacks, fire-control towers, and superstructure. Scaffolding is still present around the forward fire-control tower. It appears that the main-battery directors are mounted and under covers on the tops of the fire-control towers.

Iowa is viewed from the port side of the forward end of the superstructure on January 15, 1943. The structure with the oval plan toward the right is the top of the conning tower, the heavily armored tower that provided protected space for commanding and navigating the ship during battle. In the conning tower one level below the exposed top of the structure is the pilot house, also designated the ship and flag conning station, surrounded on three sides by the navigating bridge. The roofs of Turrets 1 and 2 are not yet completed, and awnings are erected over them to keep out the elements. Note the left sides of the rangefinders jutting from the rears of the sides of the gun houses of the 16-inch turrets.

The *Iowa* is viewed from the port side, nearly abeam the rear of the superstructure facing aft, on January 15, 1943. To the far left is the aft fire-control tower, with the aft main-battery director under cover. Several levels below and aft of that director is the turret-shaped aft Mk.37 director, for the remote control of the 5-inch/.38-caliber guns of the secondary battery.

CHAPTER 3

Commissioning and Shakedown

On February 22, 1943, although not yet quite complete, Iowa was ready to be commissioned, becoming for the first time, USS *Iowa*. Like the launching ceremony, the commissioning proceedings lacked some of the pomp normally associated with such functions. *Iowa* had begun when the threat of war was imminent, but was born to a nation at war. Indeed, the very scenario which was instrumental in the design of a "fast battleship" had begun to play out. With the crew aboard and, in some cases, working alongside the shipyard technicians the final details were finished, and following a March 1943 inclining experiment a (test done to determine a vessels stability and center of gravity) on April 1, *Iowa* left on her shakedown voyage. Thus began a Navy career that would span seven decades.

Military and civilian dignitaries stand to the front of a 16-inch gun turret on USS *Iowa* on February 22, 1943, on the occasion of the ship's commissioning. The commissioning of a ship marked the formal beginning of its operational service with the Navy. In a solemn ceremony, the commanding officer of the ship reads his and his crew's orders. Once commissioned, the name *Iowa* was prefaced by "USS," signifying United States Ship.
Naval History and Heritage Command

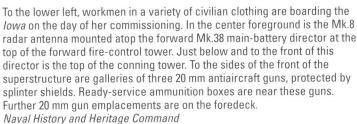

To the lower left, workmen in a variety of civilian clothing are boarding the *Iowa* on the day of her commissioning. In the center foreground is the Mk.8 radar antenna mounted atop the forward Mk.38 main-battery director at the top of the forward fire-control tower. Just below and to the front of this director is the top of the conning tower. To the sides of the front of the superstructure are galleries of three 20 mm antiaircraft guns, protected by splinter shields. Ready-service ammunition boxes are near these guns. Further 20 mm gun emplacements are on the foredeck.
Naval History and Heritage Command

Iowa is viewed from above starboard amidships facing forward on her commissioning day. The 40 mm and 5-inch guns are trained outboard and set at maximum elevation for the occasion. A cover is fitted over the tops of the uptakes on the forward smokestack. A circular work platform is on the top of the foremast; soon, an SK air-search radar antenna would be mounted over that platform. To the front of the circular work platform is the rear of the Mk.38 main-battery director; extending from its sides are the housings for the director's rangefinder. To the lower left is the front of the aft smokestack.

This photo of the *Iowa* on commissioning day was taken from above the aft smokestack. Attached to the rear of this smokestack is the mainmast, at the top of which is a small work platform with a guardrail. An SG surface-search radar antenna would soon be mounted over this platform; it was one of two SG antennas on the ship, the other being located on the front of the forward fire-control tower. To the far left, two quad 40 mm antiaircraft gun mounts have been installed inside their splinter shields, but two more 40 mm mounts are yet to be installed to each side of the forward part of the aft smokestack. The small, D-shaped tubs between the 40 mm gun mounts contained the Mk.51 directors for those mounts. *Naval History and Heritage Command*

In another view taken from above the aft smokestack, members of the commissioning crew of the *Iowa* in their dress blues are arrayed on the aft part of the main deck on commissioning day. Several batteries of 20 mm antiaircraft guns are located on the deck, within armored splinter shields: four guns diagonally situated to each side of the rear of the superstructure; two guns adjacent to each side of Turret 3; and nine guns behind a large, single splinter shield aft of Turret 3. All of these 20 mm batteries were furnished with ready-service ammunition lockers. Note that the aircraft catapults, present in January 1943, had been removed temporarily, but their drum-shaped pedestals remain in place.

This photo of the aft part of the *Iowa* on commissioning day was taken within moments of the preceding one. Mounted midway up the aft fire-control tower are two tubs for Mk.51 directors. Scaffolding with guardrails is erected around the aft Mk.37 director. On the roof of Turret Number 3 is a D-shaped platform and splinter guard for a quad 40 mm antiaircraft gun mount. The box-shaped structure on the turret roof to the front of the 40 mm gun mount is the tub for the director of that gun mount.

The commissioning crew in dress blues and invited guests are assembled on the deck of the *Iowa* during the commissioning ceremony on Washington's Birthday, February 22, 1943. Toward the left, under covers to the front of the aft fire-control tower are twin 5-inch loading machines, which were used for drilling the 5-inch gun crews on loading their pieces without having to do so in the confines of the gun houses. The drum-shaped objects on the deck in the center foreground are vents.

The commissioning ceremony is viewed from above Turret 3. In the center foreground, above the center 16-inch gun, the armored tub for the director for the 40 mm guns on the turret roof is visible. On the fantail, visible between the 16-inch guns, are two quad 40 mm gun mounts inside armored splinter shields.

A civilian operating a movie camera is standing on top of a ventilator toward the right in this view of the *Iowa*'s commissioning ceremony taken from the aft part of the main deck on February 22, 1943. All of the 5-inch and 40 mm guns are at maximum elevation for the occasion. Toward the lower left are a director tub and two hatches. The crew and civilian guests are saluting as the ship's flags are about to be hoisted.

USS *Iowa* returned to Dry Dock Number 1 at the Naval Supply Depot, Bayonne Annex, Navy Yard, New York, on March 24, 1943, to undergo inclining tests to determine the ship's stability, lightship weight, and center of gravity. Stability was tested by moving weights transversely on the ship and measuring its angles of inclination. The *Iowa* is seen in Dry Dock Number 1 on March 28.

The *Iowa* is seen from a closer perspective during inclining tests at Bayonne Annex on March 28, 1943. In the interval since the February 22 commissioning ceremony, the big, square SK air-search antenna had been mounted on top of the foremast, and Mk.4 antennas had been mounted atop the Mk.37 secondary-battery directors. Fitted between the 16-inch gun barrels and the fronts of the turrets are bucklers, also called bloomers: baggy seals to keep out the elements. The guns of Turret 2 have fabric muzzle covers.

During the March 28, 1943 inclining test, *Iowa* is viewed from amidships to the bow. In the left foreground is a gallery of four 20 mm antiaircraft guns, situated within a splinter shield attached to the deck. The shields of these guns have the type of armored shields with flared, Y-shaped openings for the guns, intended to give the gunners a better range of sight than the earlier shields, composed of two armored plates with a straight gap between them for the gun.

The starboard side of *Iowa* is viewed from amidships to the stern while dry-docked at Bayonne on March 28, 1943. In the distance above the *Iowa's* stern is the Robbins Reef Lighthouse. In addition to the Mk.37 directors with Mk.4 radar antennas located on the front and the rear of the superstructure, there was a Mk.37 director with Mk.4 antenna on each side of the smokestack. At the front of the superstructure is the conning tower, equipped with numerous vision slots on the upper, pilot house, and flag levels.

A final photograph of the *Iowa* during her March 28, 1943, inclining test reveals details of the aircraft catapults and, on the very rear of the main deck, the aircraft crane and the after 40 mm gun mounts and splinter shields, with separate tubs for these guns' directors. Note the ladder rungs running up the stern. One of the large weights used in the inclining tests is on the deck to the front of the port catapult, and another weight is being lowered into place on the port side of Turret 3.

After leaving dry dock at Bayonne, New Jersey, on March 29, 1943, the *Iowa* proceeded to Gravesend Bay off Brooklyn, New York, where she was photographed from various angles on April 4, 1943. As commissioned, the *Iowa* was painted in the Measure 22 camouflage scheme. This scheme was specified as Navy Blue (5-N) from the waterline to a horizontal line coinciding with the lowest point of the main deck; Haze Gray (5-H) on vertical surfaces above the lowest point of the main deck; and Deck Blue (20-B) on all decks and horizontal surfaces. However, as built, the *Iowa* lacked the Deck Blue paint on the wooden decks, which were unpainted.

The *Iowa* is seen from an angle more to the aft on April 4, 1943. An SG surface-search radar antenna had been mounted at the top of the mainmast attached to the aft smokestack after the ship's February 22, 1943 commissioning. Towering above the stern is the aircraft crane, for lifting scout planes from the surface of the water up to the catapults.

The battleship *Iowa* is viewed off her bow while anchored at Gravesend Bay, New York, on April 4, 1943. The line between the lower, Navy Blue paint and the Haze Gray paint is faintly visible on the hull, in line with the lowest visible point of the main deck. Seen to good effect are the prominent protrusions of the hawse pipes, through which the anchor chains are routed and in which the anchor shanks are housed when the anchors are raised.

The *Iowa* is seen from astern in Gravesend Bay on April 4, 1943. Extending from the hull are two of the boat booms, to which the ship's boats could be moored when the ship was at anchor. Each boat boom had a king post, a vertical pillar with rigging to help support the boom when in the extended position. When not in use, the boat booms, which swiveled, were stored against the hull.

USS *Iowa* is taking on supplies while anchored in Gravesend Bay on April 7, 1943. A barge is alongside the battleship on the port side, and piles of supplies are at various places on the decks. On the catapults are Vought OS2U Kingfisher scout planes, with another plane stored on the deck between the catapults. *Pacific Battleship Center*

On April 12, 1943, USS *Iowa* has departed from Gravesend Bay, New York, for sea trials and structural firing tests. She is shown underway on that date. In addition to the crew, the ship was carrying eighty officers and 242 civilian workers, temporarily assigned by the Navy Yard, New York, and the Bureau of Ships for duty during the sea trials and firing tests. From 1021 that morning until 1212 that afternoon, all guns aboard the ship were subjected to structural test firing. This firing continued at intervals in the afternoon. The *Iowa* returned to her anchorage at Gravesend Bay that night.

The forward part of USS *Iowa* is viewed from high up in her superstructure during her shakedown period in the spring of 1943. To the lower right is the Mk.4 radar antenna on top of the forward Mk.37 director. Below the antenna is a platform and tub for a 36-inch searchlight, to the front of which is the top level of the conning tower. On the roof of the conning tower are five periscope heads. The tall periscope on the raised drum at the center of the roof was designated the captain's periscope. At this point, the roof of Turret Number 2 was clear of antiaircraft gun mounts. Note the unpainted wooden decks at this point in time. *Naval History and Heritage Command*

On the foredeck of the *Iowa* as originally configured were seven 20 mm antiaircraft guns. These were located between the breakwater and the wildcats (i.e., the chain-handling wheels of the anchor windlasses) and comprised five guns within one large splinter shield and two guns farther forward within individual splinter shields. Seen here during one of the *Iowa*'s spring 1943 shakedown cruises is one of the 20 mm guns of the five-gun gallery. The gunner, far left, is peering through a Mk.14 lead-computing gun sight. In the foreground is part of the extensive splinter shield for those five guns. *Naval History and Heritage Command*

Like any other capital ship, the *Iowa* was subjected to a shakedown period, during which it conducted operations at sea, which would disclose any minor or major problems with the ship's structure or systems. One serious problem encountered was damage to the fire bricks in boilers. In this June 19, 1943, photo, bricks have fallen loose in superheat side boiler number 3 in Fire Room Number 2. The view is toward the chamber's outer-rear corner.

The aft smokestack of the *Iowa* is emitting thick, black smoke during a shakedown cruise around May 1943. Visible on the top of the mainmast is the aft SG surface-search radar antenna. In the foreground is a quad 40 mm antiaircraft gun mount; above and to the rear of the mount is the tub for a Mk.51 director. In the left foreground is a bin holding a floater net, a buoyant net that would float to the surface should the ship be sunk, providing something for survivors to cling to and remain afloat.
Naval History and Heritage Command

In this elevated view of the *Iowa* facing aft taken around May 1943, the same quad 40 mm gun mount seen in the preceding photograph is at the bottom center. Two more 40 mm mounts and splinter shields are immediately aft of this gun mount. On the side of the smokestack is a platform for a searchlight, below which is a tub for a Mk.51 director.

A view from the afterdeck of the *Iowa* during a spring 1943 shakedown cruise provides details of the face of Turret 3, including the bucklers and the four ladders for accessing the roof of the turret. In the foreground are various ventilators and several open hatches. *Naval History and Heritage Command*

In a photograph taken from the foremast of USS *Iowa* in Hampton Roads during a visit to Norfolk, Virginia, in early May 1943, some details of the front of the aft smokestack are visible, including the ladder to the catwalk between the searchlight platforms. Footrails and handrails are situated on the upper part of the smokestack to enable sailors access to that area when necessary. Also in view are details of the mainmast, including the aft SG surface-search antenna, partially in view at the top of the photo. The carrier in the background is thought to have been USS *Lexington* (CV-16). *Naval History and Heritage Command*

CHAPTER 4
USS *Iowa* Goes to War

One of the painful lessons that the US Navy learned on December 7, 1941, was that the antiaircraft defenses of the nation's warships were woefully inadequate. The size, number, and quality of such guns needed to be upgraded. While *Iowa*'s twenty 5-inch, 38-caliber dual-purpose rifles arranged in ten twin mounts were formidable, they were augmented by fifteen of the new quadruple-mount 40 mm Bofors autocannons. Also part of the original outfitting of the ship were sixty 20 mm Oerlikon autocannons in free-swinging mounts. Even before *Iowa* joined the active fleet, this installation was deemed inadequate and she returned to the builders yard for the addition of four more 40 mm mounts at the expense of eight 20 mm mounts.

Shortly after this work was complete, *Iowa* had the misfortune of scraping the bottom in Casco Bay, Maine, forcing the ship to put into the Boston Navy Yard for repair. While there, the navigating bridge was rebuilt for better weather protection. Repairs complete, *Iowa* then sailed for Newfoundland. Upon return, and after a two-week maintenance period in New York, she then ventured south to Chesapeake Bay on a covert mission to take President Roosevelt as well as most of the Nation's military leadership to Mers El Kébir, Algeria. This was the longest leg of the journey to the Tehran Conference. In order to accommodate the wheelchair-bound president, two elevators were installed on the battleship as she lay at anchor in the bay. At the same time, a bathtub was installed, although counter to legend this was not the first or only bathtub ever fitted to a battleship.

While on this voyage, one of the escorting vessels, the destroyer USS *William D. Porter* (DD-579) was conducting torpedo drills, using the imposing form of the *Iowa* as mock target for sighting. Inadvertently, *Porter* actually launched a torpedo at the battleship. Immediately alerting *Iowa* of the mistake, the giant battleship executed a hard turn avoiding the torpedo, which exploded in her wake.

Iowa returned the presidential party to the United States in December, and the elevators were subsequently removed, although the bathtub remains in place to this day.

The following month *Iowa* left the Atlantic, transiting the Panama Canal on January 7, en route to join the Pacific fleet, where she would remain for the duration of World War II.

As part one of the ships screening the Fast Carrier Task Force attacking Truk on February 19, 1944, *Iowa* encountered the Japanese light cruiser *Katori*. At a range of 14,500 yards, *Iowa* opened fire on the Japanese vessel, and proceeded to close the range while pounding the ship with forty-six 16-inch high-explosive rounds and 124 5-inch rounds. The second salvo was recorded as a hit, and after the fourth salvo the cruiser suddenly listed to port, exposing seven large shell holes, reportedly each five feet in diameter, as well as numerous smaller holes, in the starboard side. Eleven minutes after *Iowa* first hurled shells at *Katori*, the Japanese cruiser sank stern-first.

The next month *Iowa* was not so fortunate, when while participating in the bombardment of Mili Atoll in the Marshall Islands, turret two was struck by a 6-inch Japanese shell; shell fragments wounded two men nearby. Shortly thereafter a second such shell hit the hull, port side, about four feet below the main deck. At least ten more enemy near-misses were recorded.

Thereafter *Iowa* supported or participated in raids on Hollandia, Wake, Ponape, Saipan, and Tinian. During the Battle of the Philippine Sea, June 19, *Iowa*'s gunners downed three enemy aircraft, with a fourth added to the tally shortly thereafter.

From June 17 to July 10, 1943, USS *Iowa* received a post-shakedown overhaul and upgrades to her antiaircraft armaments at the Navy Yard, New York. The following series of photos was taken one day before the ship's departure from New York at the end of its period at the Navy Yard. This view offers a clear look at the quad 40 mm antiaircraft gun mounts on the stern as well as the aircraft crane.

The starboard side of the *Iowa* is shown between Turret 2 and Turret 3. Two of the new additions installed during the June-July 1943 overhaul was the quad 40 mm antiaircraft gun mount and splinter shield on the roof of Turret 2 and the elimination of four 20 mm guns on each side of the rear of the superstructure in favor of a quad 40 mm gun mount. Note the basket on the rear of the splinter shield containing a floater net. In the interim since the March 1943 photos of the ship were taken, a dark-colored canvas awning had been installed on tubular supports above the navigating bridge.

Iowa continued moving toward Japan, supporting operations against Palaus, Guam, Peleliu, and Luzon. But on December 18, *Iowa* would face a new adversary as Typhoon Cobra swept over *Iowa*, along with the rest of Task Force 38. While the storm sank three destroyers and severely damaged a cruiser, three aircraft carriers, and three additional destroyers, *Iowa* was relatively unscathed. One of her Kingfisher observation aircraft was swept overboard and lost due to the storm, and more seriously, there was damage to propeller shafts 2 and 3.

The 40 mm gun mount on the roof of Turret 3, a feature on the ship as built, is viewed from the rear with the turret trained to port. The massive hoods for the rangefinder objectives protrude from the sides of the gun house of the turret. Four baskets with flotation nets are on the rear of the gun house, as is an access ladder for the 40 mm gun mount. To the front of the bottom of that ladder, on the underside of the overhang of the gun house, is the open hatch door that provided access to the turret officer's booth.

The quad 40 mm gun mount on the roof of Turret Number 3 is seen from the rear with the turret trained aft. The gun shield had an open rear, offering splinter protection from the front and sides only. Canvas covers are fitted over the gun receivers and automatic feeds. Two curved spent-cartridge deflectors are to the rear of each gun. Around the sides and front of the pit below the gun mount are two curved holders for 40 mm ammunition.

The same 40 mm gun mount seen in the preceding photo is viewed from another angle, showing the front of the guns and their shield. Overspray from the Haze Gray paint applied to the splinter shield of the gun mount is visible on the deck planks adjacent to the shield.

This is one of the two quad 40 mm gun mounts installed to the sides of the rear of the superstructure of the *Iowa* in June–July 1943, each one replacing a gallery of four 20 mm antiaircraft guns behind splinter shields. This mount is the one on the port side, facing aft. Inside the splinter shield are four rows of 40 mm ammunition racks. On the inboard side of the splinter shield is the access door to the gun mount.

The cluster of three quad 40 mm antiaircraft gun mounts, at the upper center and left between the forward (right) and aft (left) smokestacks of the *Iowa*, is viewed from the starboard side at the Navy Yard, New York, on July 9, 1943. Below those mounts, between the two twin 5-inch gun mounts, are two tiers of 20 mm antiaircraft guns. Note the dark-colored swatches of touch-up primer at various places on the superstructure and the splinter shields.

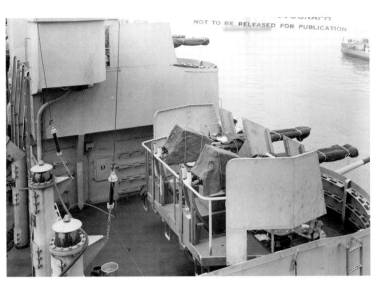

Two quad 40 mm gun mounts high up on the port side of the superstructure of the *Iowa* are shown here. To the lower left are several radio-antenna trunks, to which were attached the lower ends of the lead-ins from the wire antennas above. Ceramic entrance insulators were at the tops of these trunks, and access doors were on the sides of the trunks. At the top left is a Mk.51 director tub.

A gallery of three 20 mm antiaircraft gun mounts was positioned obliquely on the main deck abreast the front of the superstructure and Turret 2 on the *Iowa*, as seen in a July 9, 1943, photograph. On the gun house roof is a new upgrade: a gallery of three 20 mm antiaircraft guns within a splinter shield. To the rear of that gallery is the conning tower, with several men standing on the navigating bridge. On top of the conning tower is another new addition: a Mk.3 radar antenna.

A radio direction-finder (RDF) loop antenna was located at frame 97 one level above the pilot house. The vertical objects with dark-colored covers are the elevated barrels of a quad 40 mm gun mount. To the left is the front of the forward fire-control tower. Between the ladder rungs is a telephone set.

The newly emplaced 20 mm gun mounts on the roof of Turret 2 somewhat restricted the view from the vision slots in the flag level of the conning tower, as seen from this angle facing aft. On the conning tower one level above the flag level are the navigating bridge and the pilot house. Note the curve in the upper part of the bulwark of the navigating bridge, to deflect wind. The upper level of the conning tower, designated Spot 3, housed a Mk.40 main-battery director, which included three periscopes and a Mk.3 radar. Note the two periscopes on the turret roof to the front of the splinter shield; on the roof next to them are holders for the periscope covers.

The center and right 20 mm antiaircraft gun mounts atop Turret 2 are viewed from above. On the tops of the gun shields are marked "Gun 12/Group 6" (left) and "Gun 11/Group 6" (right). To the rear of the guns are 20 mm ready-service ammunition lockers. To the lower right is a stowed flotation net.

A gallery of three obliquely placed 20 mm antiaircraft guns on the main deck to the port side of the front of the superstructure is the subject of this July 9, 1943, photograph taken at the Navy Yard, New York. The hand wheels on the left sides of the pedestals of the gun mounts were for raising and lowering the gun cradle; it was raised when the gunner was aiming the piece at high elevations, and lowered for lower elevations.

The main deck of the *Iowa* is viewed facing forward from atop Turret 2 on July 9, 1943. The antiaircraft artillery arrangements on the foredeck recently had been redesigned. The battery of five 20 mm antiaircraft guns within a large splinter shield to the front of the breakwater had been removed and was replaced by two quad 40 mm mounts and Mk.51 directors with splinter shields. The two single 20 mm gun mounts and splinter shields just aft of the wildcats remained in place. On the forecastle, there now were two 20 mm gun mounts, protected by a semi-circular splinter shield. In the background is a utility ship converted from a warship of Spanish-American War vintage.

The same three 20 mm guns shown in the top right photo are viewed from farther forward on the main deck. On the top of each side of the armored shield for each gun is a dark-colored band with the gun's number and group painted on it. The closest shield is marked "Gun 6/Group 4." Under each gun receiver is a dark-colored bag for collecting spent cartridge cases. The 20 mm guns of the ship were numbered consecutively from front to rear, with even numbers on the starboard side and odd numbers on the port side.

The two quad 40 mm gun mounts and shields installed on the foredeck in the June–July 1943 modernization of the *Iowa* are to the left in this view from the starboard side of the ship, dated July 9, 1943. Toward the right are the two 20 mm antiaircraft gun mounts and shields that were part of the ship's original armaments. Ready-service ammunition lockers are to the front and rear of the splinter shields for the 20 mm antiaircraft gun mounts.

The 20 mm gun platform on the forecastle of the *Iowa*, installed in the June–July 1943, refit, is viewed from the rear. The gun shields are marked "Gun 1/ Group 1" (right) and "Gun 2/Group 2" (left). Ready-service ammunition lockers are to the rear of the platform. In the foreground are the upper ends of the hawse pipes.

USS Iowa Data	
Builder	New York Navy Yard
Laid Down	June 27, 1940
Launched	August 27, 1942
Commissioned	February 22, 1943
Decommissioned	March 24, 1949
Recommissioned	August 25, 1951
Decommissioned	February 24, 1958
Recommissioned	April 28, 1984
Decommissioned	October 26, 1990
Struck	March 17, 2006
Class	*Iowa*
Sponsor	Ilo Wallace
Displacement, standard	45,000 tons
Displacement, full load 1945	57,540 tons
Displacement, full load 1988	57,500 tons
Length, water line, full load	860 feet
Length, overall	887 feet, 2¾ inches
Beam, water line, full load	108 feet, 2 inches
Beam, maximum	109 feet 6¼ inches
Design Draft	34 feet, 9¼ inches
Bunker Fuel	6,835 tons
Endurance (design)	14,890 nautical miles @ 15 knots
Boilers	8 Babcock and Wilcox, 565 psi
Machinery	4 General Electric geared turbines, 212,000 total shaft horsepower
Speed	33 knots
Armor	12.2″ belt; 5″ on 50 lbs, armor deck; 60 lbs bomb deck; 11.2″ bulkheads; 17.3″ conning tower; 17.3″ barbettes; 17″ gun houses.
Armament, February 1943	9 16″/50 in three triple turrets, 20 dual 5″/38 gun mounts; 14 quad 40 mm mounts; 60 20 mm mounts.
Armament, July 1943	9 16″/50 in three triple turrets, 20 dual 5″/38 gun mounts; 19 quad 40 mm mounts; 52 20 mm mounts.
Armament, April 1955	9 16″/50 in three triple turrets, 20 dual 5″/38 gun mounts; 19 quad 40 mm mounts.
Armament, April 1984	9 16″/50 in three triple turrets, 12 dual 5″/38 gun mounts; 32 BGM-109 Tomahawk; 16 RGM-84 Harpoon; 4 20 mm CIWS.
Crew as designed	117 officers, 1,804 enlisted.
Crew 1945	151 officers, 2,637 enlisted.
Crew 1988	65 officers, 1,445 enlisted.

In a July 9, 1943, photo of the starboard side of the bow of USS *Iowa*, the shape of the side of the splinter shield for two 20 mm guns on the forecastle is visible. Numerous paint touch-ups of different shades than the original paint are visible on the hull. The ship's number, 61, has been painted in small, white numerals on the side of the bow.

On July 16, 1943, at 1725 in the afternoon, while maneuvering through channels in Casco Bay, Maine, the *Iowa*'s hull struck bottom. The damage was on the port side of the hull and included several holes, dents, ruptured seams, and scrapes in the shell, as well as damage to a number of fuel-oil tanks. Despite the damage, *Iowa* was able to complete her scheduled exercises in Casco Bay before reporting to the Navy Yard Annex, Boston, for repairs on July 20. This photo, taken in dry dock in Boston while repairs were underway, shows the damage to the port side of the hull. At the bottom of the photo are the keel blocks that supported the hull while in dry dock.

A "bucket brigade" is swabbing the foredeck of USS *Iowa* at some point following her June–July 1943, overhaul, as indicated by the presence of the quad 40 mm gun mounts in the background. In the foreground is the breakwater, on the rear side of which are several reels of water hoses.

USS *Iowa* underwent three weeks of maintenance, modifications, and repairs in Dry Dock Number 3 at the South Boston Naval Annex in Massachusetts from July 25 to August 16. This aerial view shows the *Iowa* at far left in Dry Dock Number 3. The *Essex*-class carrier USS *Bunker Hill* (CV-17) is at a pier to the right of the *Iowa*. The engineer officer's report for the *Iowa*'s dry-docking noted that the propellers and their shafts were in generally good condition, but that the port inboard and the starboard inboard propellers both exhibited slight dents on the leading edges of all five blades approximately four feet from the hubs.

In this bow-on view, USS *Iowa* is riding at anchor in Boston Harbor after a period of maintenance and improvements at South Boston Naval Annex that ended on August 16, 1943. Several noticeable changes had been made to the forward part of the superstructure: the sides of the deck between the forward Mk.37 director and the conning tower one level above the pilot house had been extended outward, providing some overhead cover for the navigating bridge below; the sides of the navigating bridge (but not the front) had been rebuilt, with window-style frames; and the searchlight tub to the front of the forward Mk.37 director was removed and a continuous platform was added from the quad 40 mm gun mounts abreast the front of the fire-control tower to the front of the forward Mk.37 director. Also, the bridge for the primary conning station, midway up the front face of the forward fire-control tower, which formerly had been only as wide as the tower, was now extended to the sides of the tower.

As seen from astern, USS *Iowa* is assisted by tugboats following her visit to the South Boston Naval Annex in the summer of 1943. Whereas in the spring of 1943, the ship's wooden decks had been unpainted, now they were wearing a fresh-looking coating of paint: no doubt the Deck Blue (20-B) specified for the Measure 22 camouflage scheme. The other horizontal exterior surfaces of the ship, such as the turret roofs and metal decks, also were painted Deck Blue. The smokestack caps were painted black.

In this aerial view of the *Iowa* in Boston Harbor in the summer of 1943, the contrast is very noticeable between the new Deck Blue paint on the horizontal surfaces and the Haze Gray on the vertical surfaces above the lowest point of the main deck. On the roof of Turret 1, the dark areas on the outboard sides appear to have been temporarily stowed hawsers or hoses.

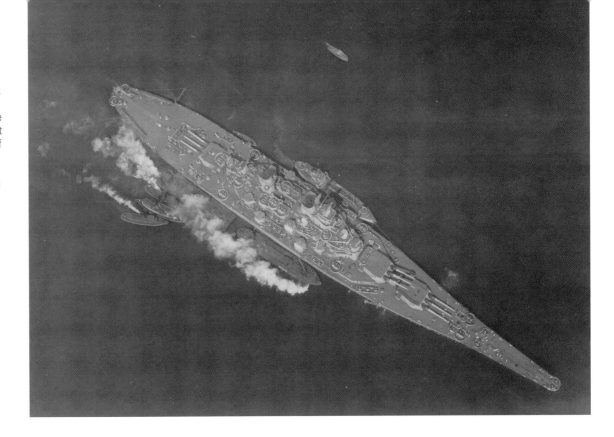

Her repairs and maintenance at the South Boston Naval Annex completed, the *Iowa* is anchored in President Roads in Boston Harbor on August 28, 1943. The following day, the ship would depart from Boston for Placentia Sound, Argentia, Newfoundland, where she would stand by ready to do battle with the German battleship *Tirpitz* should that ship leave Norwegian waters to conduct a raid in the North Atlantic: a showdown that never transpired.

USS *Iowa* cruises on Chesapeake Bay on November 12, 1943. At 0916 on that date, the battleship took aboard President Franklin D. Roosevelt and his party, bound for Oran, Algeria, en route to the Tehran Conference. The contrast between the Navy Blue below the lowest point of the main deck and the Haze Gray above that point is quite pronounced.

This close-up crop of the preceding photograph shows two tall, box-shaped elevators installed especially for the use of President Roosevelt, who suffered from polio and was largely confined to a wheelchair. The elevators provided him with access from the main deck to his quarters on the first superstructure deck and to the flag level. The elevator to the first superstructure deck is between the first and the second starboard twin 5-inch/.38-caliber gun mounts; the elevator to the flag level is faintly visible between the raised guns of the forward twin 5-inch gun mount. These elevators and other things necessary for the president's comfort and convenience were installed by the ship's force and workmen from the Navy Yard, Norfolk, while the *Iowa* was anchored in Chesapeake Bay beginning on November 7, 1943. *Pacific Battleship Center*

This photo of USS *Iowa* was taken at an unidentified harbor during the time it was assigned to transporting President Roosevelt in November and December 1943. It may have been taken at Mers-el-Kabir near Oran, Algeria, but, for its safety, the ship also visited the ports of Bahia, Brazil, and Freetown, Sierra Leone, British West Africa, before steaming to Dakar, French West Africa, where FDR rejoined the ship following the Tehran Conference. Thus, it is possible one of these ports was the scene of this photograph. The two elevators installed for the president's use are visible to each side of the forwardmost 5-inch gun mount. As in the preceding photograph, all of the 40 mm and 5-inch guns in the photo are set at maximum elevation. Alongside the hull amidships, a motor whaleboat is being hoisted. *Pacific Battleship Center*

The port of Mers-el-Kabir near Oran, Algeria, the initial destination of President Franklin D. Roosevelt on his trip to the Tehran Conference in late 1943, is seen from the ship that transported him there, the USS *Iowa*. A number of distinguished civilian and military leaders accompanied Roosevelt on the ship, including FDR's confidante Harry Hopkins; ADM William D. Leahy; chief-of-staff Gen. George C. Marshall; ADM Ernest J. King, commander-in-chief of the US Fleet; and Gen. Henry H. "Hap" Arnold.

President Franklin D. Roosevelt delivers an address from the deck of USS *Iowa* with one of the 16-inch turrets in the background and several 20 mm guns to the right. This may have been the occasion of FDR's farewell talk to the ship's crew, in which he noted that, "from all I have seen and all I have heard, the *Iowa* is a 'happy ship,' and having served with the Navy for many years, I know—and you know—what that means. It is part and parcel of what we are trying to do, to make every ship happy and efficient."
Pacific Battleship Center

While shelling Japanese coastal defenses on Mili Atoll in the Marshall Islands on the morning of March 18, 1944, USS *Iowa* suffered several shell hits from shore batteries. The first hit, a shell of approximately six inches in diameter, struck the left side of Turret 2 about eighteen inches above the top of the barbette, detonating on impact, as seen in this photo included in the official report of the mission. *Naval History and Heritage Command*

About five minutes after Turret 2 of the *Iowa* was hit, another Japanese shell penetrated the port side of the hull near frame 134 about four feet below the main deck, causing a hole in the shell about 30 inches by 50 inches. A torpedo bulkhead inside the hull prevented this shell from penetrating the interior of the ship. Damage also was done to two degaussing coils running along this part of the hull.

In addition to the damage the Japanese shell did to the side of Turret 2, the blast also tore off approximately twenty feet of the watershed and gas seal on the left side of that turret, as seen here. Also, fragments from the blast broke through the window for the left pointer's sight, injuring two crewmen inside the turret.

The hole in the shell of the hull from a Japanese projectile on March 18, 1944, is viewed from within compartment B-226V, a void space at frame 134. At the lower right, a hand is holding a ruler for reference. The two cables in the view are the two damaged degaussing coils. *Naval History and Heritage Command*

Members of the *Iowa*'s crew attend mass on the quarterdeck around the time of the June 1944, Marianas Campaign. The Measure 32 camouflage as modified with the hard edges between the Light Gray (5-L) and Navy Blue (5-N) areas is seen to good advantage. The objects on the front of the splinter shield for the 40 mm gun mount on the turret are crew helmets, painted Light Gray. *Naval History and Heritage Command*

In a photograph dated December 11, 1944, USS *Iowa* is underway in moderately rough seas. If the date of this photo is correct, on that date the ship, heading up Task Group 34.5 (Special Group), departed from its anchorage at Ulithi Atoll Lagoon to join Task Group 38.2, Third Fleet, bound for a raid against Luzon in the Philippines.

On the return voyage from Luzon, on December 23, 1944, the number 3 main engine was shut down due to excessive vibration in the shaft. After *Iowa* arrived at Ulithi, divers discovered damage to the number 3 shaft at its strut bearing. To effect repairs, *Iowa* steamed on three propellers to a floating dry dock at Seeadler Harbor, Manus Island, Papua New Guinea. While en route, the *Iowa* developed excessive vibration in propeller shaft 2. The battleship is shown entering the Floating Dry Dock ABSD-2 on December 27, 1944. Note the heavily weathered hull, with significant paint erosion in evidence.

The superstructure of the *Iowa* is partially visible above the top of floating dry dock ABSD-2 on December 27, 1944. The floating dry dock consisted of two massive "walls" called wings, attached at the bottom to transverse, floodable pontoons, the tops of which constituted a platform upon which the *Iowa* rested. The *Iowa* entered ABSD-2 while the pontoons were flooded and submerged. Once positioned between the wings, the water was pumped out of the pontoons, causing them to rise until the platform with the ship resting on it was above water. ABSD-2 was equipped with a massive, traveling crane atop each wing. The stern of the *Iowa* is visible between the rears of the wings to the right.

USS *Iowa* has advanced farther into Floating Dry Dock ABSD-2, affording a close view of the two quad 40 mm gun mounts and their adjoining director tubs on the foredeck. Some of the details that are visible in the photo include the open vision-port covers on the front of the forward Mk.37 secondary battery director and the crewmen sunning themselves on the director's roof; the stack of three life rafts next to the 40 mm gun mount on the first level of the superstructure; and the awning over the platform to the front of the foundation of the forward Mk.37 director.

The *Iowa* is seen from the port side while undergoing repairs in Floating Dry Dock ABSD-2 on December 28, 1944. The forecastle is visible above the top of the port wing of the dry dock toward the left, while the stern and the aircraft crane of the battleship protrude to the rear of the dry dock to the right.

Iowa is viewed facing the bow in floating dry dock on December 28, 1944. Several barges, including one with a two-story structure on it, are moored across the front end of the dry dock. The splinter shield for two 20 mm guns on the forecastle and the SG surface-search radar antenna at the top of the foremast are visible.

Once in dry dock, the reasons for the excessive vibration in propeller shaft 3 became apparent. This shaft had dropped three inches in its bearing, the number 3 main strut bearing had been ground down to the depth of an inch, and the propeller boss gland and stud nuts had been wiped off. Other damage had been done to shaft and strut components.

Naval personnel are lined up on the rear of the platform of ABSD-2, viewing the work on the propellers of USS *Iowa* on December 28, 1944. The frame-type structure on the rear of the floating dry dock is a swing bridge: there were four of these assemblies, two to the front of the floating dry dock and two to the rear, and when a pair of them was swung together, they formed a walkway across the dry dock, or, in this case, a walkway to the stern of the ship.

Damage to the bearing of propeller 3 of USS *Iowa* is shown close up on December 28, 1944. The propellers of the ship were numbered 1 to 4 from starboard to port. Propeller 3 was the inboard port propeller.

Navy personnel are removing propeller 3 from its bearing on December 28, 1944. They are using a compound system of chain hoists hooked to fittings welded to the hull to effect this task. Once the propeller was freed from the shaft and bearing, it would be hoisted to the main deck, where it would be stored until a permanent fix was made, presumably while the ship underwent extensive repairs and modifications at Hunters Point Naval Shipyard, San Francisco, California, from January to February 1945.

USS *Iowa* is viewed from astern in this aerial view taken during the ship's time in the floating dry dock at Seeadler Harbor, Papua New Guinea, in late December 1944. Surrounding the floating dry dock are numerous barges and craft.

Floating Dry Dock ABSD-2, in which the *Iowa* underwent inspections for propeller problems at Seeadler Harbor, was a sectional dry dock, comprising ten units designated sections A through J. Each section had a pontoon with two wing sections on it. When assembled together, the sections made up a unified floating dry dock large enough to handle even the battleship *Iowa*. The tops of the ten pontoons are visible on the outboard sides of the wings in these aerial photos.

Floating Dry Dock ABSD-2 was built at Mare Island Navy Yard, California, and towed in sections to Seeadler Harbor. It had a lifting capacity of 100,000 tons, well exceeding USS *Iowa*'s full-load displacement of 57,500 tons. ABSD-2 remained at Seeadler Harbor long after the end of World War II and was decommissioned in 1987. Its wreckage reportedly still exists off Lombrum Point, Manus Island.

From January 16 to March 18, 1945, USS *Iowa* visited the San Francisco Naval Shipyard at Hunters Point for repairs, maintenance, and modernization. The ship is seen here near the end of that time, testing its systems on San Francisco Bay on March 5, 1945. During its period at Hunters Point, the ship's navigating bridge was fully enclosed with windshields across the front and along the sides of the pilot house, similar to the navigating bridges on *Iowa*'s sister ships *Missouri* and *Wisconsin*. In addition, on the level above the navigating bridge, a platform with a bulwark was extended around the front of the conning tower.

USS *Iowa* cruises at low speed on San Francisco Bay on March 5, 1945. By now, the *Iowa* had traded in its Vought Kingfisher scout planes for Curtiss SC-1 Seahawks, single-seat seaplanes introduced to the fleet in late 1944. A Curtiss SC-1 is on each catapult, and a third one is stored on the deck between the catapults.

Another significant and highly visible change that had been made to USS *Iowa* during her period of time at Hunters Point in early 1945, was her return to Measure 22 camouflage: the scheme in which the ship had begun her career. The earlier version of Measure 22 on the *Iowa* established the lowest part of the demarkation line between the Navy Blue (5-N) and the lighter Haze Gray (5-H) at a lower point than in the 1945 application of the scheme. Thus, in 1945, there was not a thin band of Haze Gray on the upper part of the rear of the hull: there was Haze Gray on the hull only from abeam Turret 1 to the bow.

USS *Iowa* is viewed from off her port bow in this March 5, 1945, aerial photograph. The redesigned navigating bridge and platform above it, results of the January-March 1945, renovations at Hunters Point, gave the front of the superstructure a boxy look but also a more finished appearance, and these new features improved the comfort and safety of personnel using them.

The *Iowa* rides at anchor off Hunters Point on March 18, 1945, the day of her departure from that Navy Yard. While the ship was at Hunters Point, a new foremast was installed, with a topmast holding a new SU surface-search radar antenna in a radome. The SK air-search antenna was retained for now on the foremast, to the front of the SU antenna. The mainmast was redesigned, with stronger supporting struts and a topmast that held the aft SG surface-search antenna. An SR air-search antenna now was installed on the maintop. The ship's number, 61, is painted in white aft of the anchor.

The new masts and radar installations are faintly visible in this March 18, 1945 view of the *Iowa* off Hunters Point. Another modernization made to the ship during the time spent at Hunters Point was the addition of the Mk.12/22 radar antennas to the tops of the Mk.37 secondary-battery directors. The Mk.12 antenna was similar in appearance to the directors' original Mk.4 antennas; the Mk.22 parabolic antenna, mounted to the right side of the Mk.12 antenna, was sometimes called the "orange peel" antenna because of its curved shape.

In the last of a series of photos of USS *Iowa* off Hunters Point on March 18, 1945, Curtiss SC-1 scout planes are mounted on both catapults. The one on the port side has the number 73 on the fuselage in white, while the one on the starboard catapult is numbered 71. On the deck between the catapults is a third SC-1 with its wings folded.

The *Iowa*, right, undergoes an underway replenishment from USS *Cahaba* (AO-82), an *Escambia*-class replenishment oiler, along with the carrier USS *Shangri-La* (CV-38), left, in the Pacific Ocean on July 8, 1945. The *Iowa* had just finished refueling two USN ships when she came alongside *Cahaba* at 0716 that morning and quickly began taking on fuel herself. It was a unique situation when an oiler simultaneously conducted an underway replenishment (UNREP) of two ships.

The structures forward of the forward fire-control tower are the focus of this photo of the *Iowa* undergoing an UNREP from USS *Cahaba* on July 8, 1945. The operation was performed at a speed of 10 knots and a course of 240 degrees.

The folded wing of one of USS *Shangri-La*'s SB2C Helldivers is visible to the left in this photo of the UNREP of USS *Iowa* on July 8, 1945. The fuel lines rigged from the replenishment oiler USS *Cahaba* to the *Iowa* are clearly visible. The total refueling process on this date took about five hours.

A final photo of the *Iowa* taken from USS *Shangri La* while taking on fuel from USS *Cahaba* on July 8, 1945, focuses on the area from Turret 3 to the starboard catapult, including a view of a Curtiss SC-1 Seahawk on the catapult and another one stored on the deck. Gathered under the 16-inch guns is a seated audience listening to music provided by the ship's band. The *Iowa* completed her UNREP at approximately 1220 and then resumed her normal operations with her task group.

On July 24, 1945, US carrier-based aircraft attacked the Japanese naval base at Kure with great success, destroying and heavily damaging a number of warships, including the battleship *Hyūga*. On the following day, a scout plane from USS *Iowa* photographed the *Hyūga* where it rested, partially sunk and amidships awash, in Kure harbor.

The USN aerial attacks on Kure continued through July 28, 1945, on which date a scout aircraft from USS *Iowa* took this photograph of the ships in the harbor under assault. The focus of the photo at the lower center is the battleship *Ise*, which was hit by five 1,000-pound bombs and eleven smaller bombs on that date, sinking in shallow water.

This rare scene of sister ships USS *Iowa*, left, and USS *Missouri*, right, steaming closely together, was photographed in August 1945, while the ships were en route to Tokyo Bay for the Japanese surrender. The purpose of the close-formation maneuver was to transfer by highline a landing party of armed bluejackets from the *Missouri* to the *Iowa*. In the background is an *Essex*-class fleet aircraft carrier. *Iowa* still had her square-shaped SK air-search radar antenna on the foretop, while *Missouri* had a dish-type SK-2 radar antenna.

The *Iowa*, right, and the *Missouri* are viewed from the front during the personnel-transfer operation off the coast of Japan in August 1945. By this point in the war, both ships had similarly designed navigating bridges. Among some of the differences in the ships were that the *Missouri* had a quad 40 mm gun mount on the roof of Turret 2, while the *Iowa* had a gallery of three 20 mm antiaircraft guns atop its Turret 2. *Navy History and Heritage Command*

In a photo taken from USS *Missouri* in Tokyo Bay on September 2, 1944, small boats are bringing Allied representatives to the surrender ceremony on that ship while her sister ship, USS *Iowa*, lies at anchor in the distance. The *Iowa* would remain at anchor at Berth Fox 72 in the center of Tokyo Bay through September 19, departing for Okinawa and ultimately the United States on September 20, 1945.

CHAPTER 5
Peacetime

After briefly anchoring in Tokyo Bay as part of the occupying force, *Iowa* took aboard liberated prisoners as well as troops with orders home, and sailed for the United States via Pearl Harbor as part of the Magic Carpet operation. Here, *Iowa* is in the foreground with *Colorado* BB-45 (far left) and *West Virginia* BB-48, all their decks crowded with weary yet victorious servicemen, tied up ahead of her stay at the Hawaiian base.

Following the Japanese surrender *Iowa* briefly remained in Tokyo Bay as part of the occupying force. On September 20, after taking aboard liberated US prisoners of war as well as some homeward-bound soldiers, *Iowa* steamed first for Pearl Harbor, and then the continental United States. After arriving in Seattle on October 15, she then was involved in training operations off the western coast of the United States until January 1946, when she again returned to Tokyo as flagship of the Fifth Fleet. Returning again to the San Francisco Bay area on March 25, 1946, she continued to primarily perform training duties.

Iowa entered the Puget Sound Naval Shipyard on December 1, 1947, for a routine overhaul. Departing the Yard on May 12, 1948, she returned to training duties, including an eight-week midshipman cruise beginning June 22. In July, she steamed again to Hawaiian waters, and on July 31, took part in a live fire exercise against the former battleship *Nevada*. The venerable vessel, despite having been subjected to two atomic bomb blasts during the Operation Crossroads

tests at Bikini Atoll, had stubbornly refused to sink, even when subsequently fired upon by the combined might of *Iowa* and the light cruisers *Astoria*, *Pasadena*, and *Springfield*. *Nevada* was ultimately dispatched by use of an aerial torpedo.

In September 1948, *Iowa* entered San Francisco Naval Shipyard to become part of the reserve fleet. The process, which consumed six months, being completed on March 24, 1949, saw preservatives applied to bare metals surfaces, delicate items packed away, paint touched up, and the vessel sealed and dehumidified. Cathodic protection slowed rust and deterioration of the hull.

In January 1946, USS *Iowa* was sent to Japan, where she would serve as flagship of the Fifth Fleet through March of that year. At one point during the crossing of the Pacific en route to Tokyo, the ship encountered heavy seas, as seen in this photograph taken from the bridge. Two periscope heads are visible on the roof of Turret 1; on their inboard sides are holders for the periscope covers.

On October 11, 1946, USS *Iowa* was photographed off the Puget Sound Naval Shipyard in Washington, where she was undergoing repairs and modifications. The ship has been repainted in the US Navy's postwar scheme of Haze Gray on all vertical surfaces and Deck Blue on all horizontal surfaces and decks.

The crane and aircraft catapults are visible, although the Curtiss SC-1 scout planes have not yet returned to the ship following *Iowa*'s time in the shipyard.

As seen in another October 11, 1946, photo at Puget Sound Naval Shipyard, the *Iowa* now was equipped with the dish-type SK-2 air-search radar antenna on the foretop; in this photo the antenna is trained to port. The tub that formerly held 20 mm guns on the forecastle would remain a permanent fixture of the ship.

USS *Iowa* is docked at Hunters Point Naval Shipyard on July 18, 1947. On the following day, the ship would sail for Hawaii carrying thirteen state governors as the guests of Secretary of the Navy James Forrestal. In the background is the famous traveling crane at Hunters Point, which at the time of its construction in 1947 was touted as the world's largest of its type. It had a lifting capacity of one million pounds. When built, one of its principal uses was for hoisting the big guns on battleships and even entire gun turrets. Note the Curtiss SC-1 scout planes on the catapults; the one on the starboard catapult has the code "BA" on the vertical tail and the fuselage number two, while the plane on the port catapult has no such markings.

Turrets 1 and 2 are trained to port in this photo taken in July 1947. The recently mounted, dish-type SK-2 air-search radar antenna atop the foremast is visible. The 40 mm and the 20 mm antiaircraft guns had been removed from the tubs on the foredeck. *Naval History and Heritage Command*

In a companion view to the preceding one, Turrets 1 and 2 are viewed from above while trained to port. The platform and splinter shield for three 20 mm antiaircraft guns remains on the roof of Turret 2, but the guns and their pedestals have been removed. In the foreground is the top of the conning tower and the bridge surrounding it. *Naval History and Heritage Command*

Turret 3 is trained to port in this July 1947 photograph. The rear of the forward smokestack is in the lower left corner of the photo, and the aft smokestack, with its black cap, is to the front of Turret 3. The amidships 40 mm gun mounts are still present in the foreground. Two Curtiss SC-1 scout planes are on the catapults. *Naval History and Heritage Command*

One of the *Iowa*'s two Curtiss SC-1 scout planes is being hoisted aboard during a July 1947 cruise in the Pacific. The plane was equipped with radar; note the white radome below the wing. The "BA" on the tail of the SC-1 on the port catapult pertained to Battleship Spotting Squadron 1B (VO-1B). On the main deck in the foreground are some of the ship's motorboats. *Naval History and Heritage Command*

The *Iowa* has just arrived at Pearl Harbor on August 9, 1948, as part of a task force carrying almost 2,000 Naval Reserve midshipmen from college and universities in the United States on a training cruise. The dish-shaped SK-2 air-search radar antenna had been removed from the foretop, replaced by an SR-3 radar antenna. Extensive corrosion is visible on the hull above the boot topping.

With downtown San Francisco in the background, USS *Iowa* passes under the San Francisco Bay Bridge on September 3, 1948. There, the ship would spend the next several months undergoing preparations for decommissioning at Hunters Point Naval Shipyard. A Curtiss SC-1 is on one of the catapults, and two other SC-1s with wings folded are stored on deck. *Pacific Battleship Center*

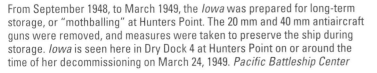

From September 1948, to March 1949, the *Iowa* was prepared for long-term storage, or "mothballing" at Hunters Point. The 20 mm and 40 mm antiaircraft guns were removed, and measures were taken to preserve the ship during storage. *Iowa* is seen here in Dry Dock 4 at Hunters Point on or around the time of her decommissioning on March 24, 1949. *Pacific Battleship Center*

From March 1949, to August 1951, the battleship *Iowa* was stored with the Pacific Reserve Fleet at San Francisco. She is seen in this February 1951, photo with other ships of the Reserve Fleet, including the carrier USS *Intrepid* (CV-11). The *Iowa* had been repainted, sealant had been applied to places where moisture could infiltrate, covers had been installed on the tops of the smokestacks, and dome-shaped shelters had been installed in the 40 mm gun tubs.

CHAPTER 6

War in Korea

When North Korea invaded South Korea on June 25, 1950, it signaled the outbreak of a war that many feared would escalate into World War III. In order to quickly counter the Communist aggression, many ships of the US reserve fleet were reactivated. Among the reactivated ships was the *Iowa*. Reactivation began on July 14, 1951, and *Iowa* was recommissioned on August 25. In March 1952, *Iowa* sailed for Korean waters.

Her combat operations against Korea began on April 8, 1952, when she shelled Communist supply lines near Wonsan-Songjin. The next day she turned her guns against enemy troop concentrations and suspected gun positions. Just under a week later *Iowa* again rained destruction on North Korean forces, demolishing six gun positions and killing one hundred enemy troops. On April 14, *Iowa* entered Wonsan Harbor and shelled railheads, warehouses, and observation posts with impunity.

On April 20, *Iowa* began firing above the 38th parallel for the first time, destroying railroad tunnels and lines and various other enemy positions. May 25 found *Iowa* off Chongjin, North Korea, a mere fifty-five miles from the Russian border, pounding various strategic targets, including rail lines and industry.

On August 20, the destroyer *Thompson* DD-627, bombarding the enemy at Sŏngjin, was hit by a Chinese artillery battery, wounding several men. *Iowa*, only sixteen miles away, and having more advanced medical facilities, took aboard nine of *Thompson*'s wounded crewmen and protected the destroyer as it withdrew.

September saw *Iowa* again firing on Wonsan, this time with Gen. Mark W. Clark, commander-in-chief of United Nations Forces in Korea, aboard as an observer. The battleship continued shore bombardments in support of Allied troops until October 17, when she sailed for Norfolk and an overhaul.

Following overhaul, *Iowa* was involved in training operations in the Caribbean, then operated as flagship of the Second Fleet, and participated in Operation Mariner, a NATO exercise in July 1953.

In June 1954, while on a midshipmen training cruise, *Iowa* rendezvoused with her sisters *New Jersey, Missouri*, and *Wisconsin* in Guantanamo Bay, Cuba. This became the only time that all four battleships of the *Iowa* class would operate together.

January 1955, saw *Iowa* steaming in the Mediterranean, visiting Gibraltar, Oran, Naples, Istanbul, Athens, and other ports. This was the first time a battleship had been in these waters since World War II. During this time a nuclear warhead for the 16-inch naval gun was developed. The Mk.23 round was a 15–20 kiloton yield weapon derived from the Army's 280 mm atomic cannon round. Modifications were made to enable the *Iowa* to store and assemble their rounds. The standard allowance was ten of the nuclear rounds and nine Mk.24 practice rounds, and a single drill projectile. Provisions for these rounds were made in the Turret 2 magazine.

Iowa would return to Cuba in April 1956, and again bring midshipmen to Guantanamo Bay in June of that year. In January 1957, she again glided through the waters of the Mediterranean and participated in the International Naval Review off Hampton Roads, Virginia, in June of that year. After participation in Operation Strike Back, and NATO operation in the North Atlantic, in September 1957, *Iowa* returned to the United States, and on February 24, 1958, was decommissioned for a second time, this time at the Philadelphia Navy Yard.

The war in Korea in the early 1950s led the US government to reconsider its retirement of many of its battleships following World War II. One of those to be reactivated was the battleship *Iowa*, shown here on July 18, 1951, one year after the commencement of the war, being towed away from its berth at the naval yard in San Francisco in advance of its recommissioning. *Pacific Battleship Center*

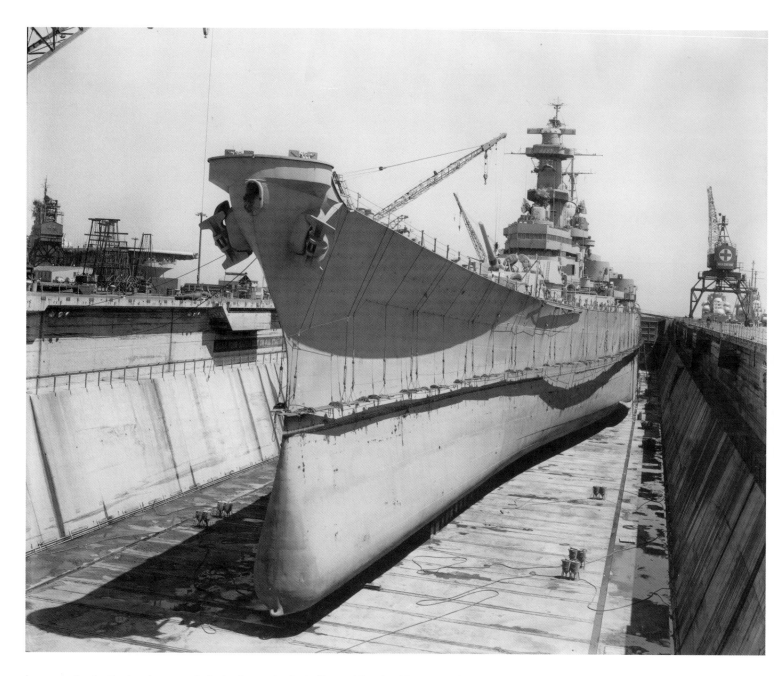

In preparation for the *Iowa*'s recommissioning for service in the Korean War, the ship was overhauled at the San Francisco Naval Shipyard, Hunters Point, in the summer of 1951. She is shown here in dry dock at Hunters Point on July 27 of that year. Of interest is the fact that the radar antennas for the Mk.38 main-battery directors were stored on the roof of Turret Number 1. The shields for two 20 mm antiaircraft guns are visible above the tub on the forecastle.

Officers, crewmen, and civilian guests on the after part of the main deck of the *Iowa* salute the colors during the battleship's recommissioning ceremony at San Francisco Naval Shipyard, California, on August 25, 1951. The *Iowa* now had a new mainmast of cantilevered design that was attached to the rear of the aft smokestack. On a platform near the top of the mainmast was an SP height-finding radar antenna.

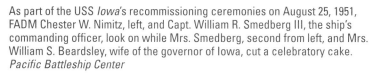

As part of the USS *Iowa*'s recommissioning ceremonies on August 25, 1951, FADM Chester W. Nimitz, left, and Capt. William R. Smedberg III, the ship's commanding officer, look on while Mrs. Smedberg, second from left, and Mrs. William S. Beardsley, wife of the governor of Iowa, cut a celebratory cake. *Pacific Battleship Center*

During the latter part of the Korean War, USS *Iowa* was the flagship of VADM Robert T. Briscoe, commander of the Seventh Fleet, operating off the coast of Korea. The battleship is seen here off communist-held Wonsan Harbor on April 18, 1952. On the aft part of the main deck is a helicopter, apparently a Sikorsky HO3S-1. In the years after World War II, helicopters increasingly became the preferred scouting and utility aircraft for battleships and smaller warships.

Elements of the new radar and communications antennas installed on the foremast of the *Iowa* during her refitting in July 1951 are visible above the Mk.38 main-battery director and its Mk.13 radar antenna. On the foremast is a new SPS-6 radar antenna with a Zenith-Search set, to the sides of which are AT-150 short-range ship-to-ship and AS-390 ship-to-air antennas, TBS radio antennas, and position lights.

The foremast of the *Iowa* is seen from the port side at San Francisco in July 1951. On the front of the foretop is the SPS-6 radar antenna, with a dual feedhorn radiator unit (for directing radar and identification friend or foe—IFF—signals to the antenna) to its front and a vane for counterbalancing the antenna against the wind to the rear. Atop the short topmast on the rear of the platform is an SG-6 surface-search radar antenna.

One of the 16-inch/50-caliber Mk.7 guns in USS *Iowa*'s Turret 2 fires a round toward a target in North Korea in mid-1952. To the front of Turret 1 are two quad 40 mm antiaircraft gun mounts and directors. The two 20 mm guns and tubs to the front of these 40 mm gun mounts that were present during World War II had been removed.

On October 14–15, 1952, USS *Iowa* bombarded enemy positions and vehicles in the vicinity of Kojo, North Korea. The *Iowa* is seen here during that bombardment. During those two days, the 16-inch/50-caliber Mk.7 guns fired a total of 351 shells, while the 5-inch/38-caliber batteries expended 2,908 rounds. Painted on the roof of Turret 1 is the ship's number, 61, underlined, while an American flag is painted on the roof of Turret 2. The October 14–15, 1952, bombardment of Kojo marked the end of the *Iowa*'s October 28, 1952, active operations in the Korean War. *US Navy*

Sister ships USS *Iowa* (foreground) and USS *Missouri* are moored together at Yokosuka, Japan, on October 19, 1952. This was the first time they were together since World War II, and the occasion was the transfer of the flag and staff of VADM Joseph J. Clark, commander, Seventh Fleet, from the *Iowa* to the *Missouri*. *US Navy*

The aft portions of the *Missouri*, foreground, and the *Iowa* can be compared in this photo from their meeting on October 19, 1952. For example, note the different construction of their aircraft cranes, with *Iowa*'s featuring solid structural members with lightening holes, while *Missouri*'s is of welded tubular construction. A large quantity of empty ammunition packing cases are piled on the main deck of *Iowa* aft of Turret 3, a result of the recent bombardment of Kojo, North Korea. *National Museum of Naval Aviation*

USS *Missouri*, left, and *Iowa* are seen from the front during the transfer of VADM Clark's command from the *Iowa* to the *Missouri* at Yokosuka on October 19, 1952. Many major and minor differences can be discerned between the two ships, such as the presence of a quad 40 mm gun mount on a raised platform on the roof of Turret 2 of the *Missouri* versus a splinter shield and low platform for 20 mm guns but with no guns mounted on the roof of Turret 2 of the *Iowa*. *National Museum of Naval Aviation*

By October 28, 1952, the *Iowa* was at Pearl Harbor, where she is seen in this aerial photo. A large number of the crew is on deck in dress whites. A clear view is available of the cantilevered mainmast attached to the rear of the aft smokestack.

Crewmen in dress whites line the rails during USS *Iowa*'s visit to Pearl Harbor on October 28, 1952. Following this visit, the *Iowa* would be reassigned to the Second Fleet in the Atlantic, and she would proceed to the Norfolk Naval Shipyard for an overhaul.

All four battleships of the *Iowa* class are present in this June 7, 1954, photograph taken in the Virginia Capes operating area. This is thought to have been the only time all four *Iowa*-class ships operated together; at the time they were with Battleship Division (BatDiv) 2. The closest ship is *Iowa* (BB-61), followed by *Wisconsin* (BB-64), *Missouri* (BB-63), and *New Jersey* (BB-62). By this time, the splinter shield or tub on the roof of Turret 2, which once had housed three 20 mm guns and had been present as late as October 1952, had been removed. *US Navy*

USS *Iowa* is docked at Pier 7 at Norfolk in November 1956, with the command light cruiser *Northampton* (CLC-1) moored alongside her. It seems that a dark-colored deck paint, probably Deck Blue, either was being applied to or removed from the wooden decks. There is an unpainted area aft of Turret 3, and much of the main deck forward of the superstructure is unpainted, save for painted areas along the port side of the deck and on the foredeck, and a swatch to the front of Turret 1.

USS *Iowa* steams on the high seas during 1956. To each side of the aft smokestack is a boat crane, installed sometime during the year between June 1954, and June 1955. The cranes consisted of a king post and a boom. The boom of the port crane is visible against the side of the aft smokestack. The king posts of the two cranes now formed a support for the mainmast structure, on the rear of the smokestack, which formerly had been of cantilevered design.

USS *Iowa* paid a visit to New York City in May 1957. Here, the battleship is proceeding past piers along the harbor. At this time, the ship's paint was in bright, ship-shape condition. The *Iowa*'s ship number, 61, is painted in large numerals on the bow in white with black shadowing.

The *Iowa* is dressed out from stem to stern as a participant in the International Naval Review at Hampton Roads, Virginia, in June 1957. Noticeable on the roof of Turret 1 is the ship's number with a line under it, both of which are painted white. The smokestack caps and the mainmast above the level of the bottom of the aft smokestack cap were painted a satin or glossy black.

Crewmen and officers in dress whites and Marines in their dress blues are lining the rails of the USS *Iowa* during the International Naval Review at Norfolk in June 1957, as a Navy helicopter banks over the ship. Held from June 11–13, 1957, at Hampton Roads, in part to honor the 350th anniversary of the founding of Jamestown, Virginia, the International Naval Review featured numerous ships of the US Navy and allied powers passing in review before President Dwight D. Eisenhower. *US Navy*

The *Iowa* is seen from above during the 1957 International Naval Review. The wooden decks were bare wood, while the horizontal surfaces, including steel decks and platforms and the roofs of the turrets, were Dark Gray Deck Type A (smooth) or Dark Gray Deck Type B (nonskid). Depending on whether the ship was painted in the Measure 27 or Measure 17 USN camouflage of the mid-1950s, the vertical surfaces of the ship would have been, respectively, Haze Gray (5-H) or Ocean Gray (5-O).

USS *Iowa* is followed by a line of warships during a cruise in August 1957. The shape of the kingpost of the port boat crane just aft of the aft smokestack is prominent, as well as the crossbeam that connected the tops of the king posts and also served as a support for the mainmast.
Naval History and Heritage Command

USS *Iowa* was decommissioned for the second time on February 2, 1958, and was consigned to the Atlantic Reserve Fleet at Philadelphia. She is seen to the far right with two of her *Iowa*-class sister battleships while in long-term storage at Philadelphia in 1967. They are, left to right, the *Wisconsin* (BB-64) and the *New Jersey* (BB-62). The following year, the *New Jersey* would be recommissioned and modernized and would be used for shore bombardment during the Vietnam War, but the *Iowa* and the *Wisconsin* would sit out that war.

When *Iowa* was decommissioned in February 1958, she joined thirteen other battleships already placed in reserve. Sister ships *Missouri* and *New Jersey* had been laid up in 1955 and 1957 respectively. Also in reserve were the four *South Dakota* class ships, both *North Carolina* class ships, the three *Colorado* class ships, and both *Tennessee* class ships. *Iowa*'s youngest sister, the *Wisconsin*, would join the mothball fleet one month after *Iowa*. While owning fifteen battleships, for the first time in the twentieth century the United States fleet would not include an active battleship.

As the years passed the older battleships were stricken from the Navy list and sold for scrap, or offered as donations at veteran's memorials. *Tennessee* and *California*, as well as *Maryland*, *Colorado*, and *West Virginia* were stricken in March 1959, and shortly thereafter all were reduced to scrap. *Washington* followed suit in June 1960, while her sister *North Carolina* was saved as a memorial. By the time the *South Dakota*s were stricken in June 1962, interest in preservation had increased, and three of the four became monuments, only *South Dakota* herself succumbing to the scrapper's torch.

With the devastating effect of 16-inch gunfire on the enemy in Korea still relatively fresh in the military mind, discarding the battleship out of hand was not considered.

During this time, however, various proposals were brought forth to convert the *Iowa*s to other configuration, ranging from guided missile launch ships to combination aircraft carrier and surface combatant, even possibly a combination fast combat support ship with bombardment capability.

While the war in Vietnam brought about the reactivation of her sister *New Jersey* in April 1968 for a brief, twenty-month period of combat operations, *Iowa* continued to sleep in Philadelphia.

By 1978, the battleship *Iowa* had been sitting idle at the Philadelphia Naval Shipyard for twenty years with little maintenance being done to preserve her. As seen in a photo taken sometime that year, the wooden decks were rotting and rust was prevalent.

Iowa is viewed from the forward port quarter at Philadelphia in April 1980. The following year, the ship would enjoy a rebirth and a restoration of her former glory. To the starboard side of the *Iowa* is the *Wisconsin*.

CHAPTER 8
Return to Service

In 1981, as part of the Reagan Administration's plan to build a 600-ship US Navy, all four battleships of the *Iowa* class were slated for modernization and reactivation. Here, tugboats are moving the *Iowa* to a new berth at Philadelphia Naval Shipyard in April 1982, preparatory to her modernization. Considerable rust is visible on the hull. *US Navy*

During the 1970s the tide began to turn against the venerable battleships, and many forces from within and outside the navy sought to have them stricken and set for disposal. Variously, Secretary of the Navy John Warner, or Chief of Naval Operations Zumwalt, or more often the Marines, who fondly recalled the effectiveness of heavy naval gunfire during amphibious operations, forced the *Iowa*s to be maintained in the reserve fleet.

During the closing years of the Carter administration, momentum began to grow in naval circles for Congress to reactivate the *Iowa*s, in large part due to the build-up of the Soviet navy and increased Soviet aggression. Feeling such reactivation would undermine peace efforts, the administration blocked all such efforts. The election of Ronald Reagan to the nation's highest office not only removed the biggest hurdle from the reactivation efforts, but also brought with it a new champion for the cause in the form of new Secretary of the Navy John F. Lehman, Jr.

While the most recently used *New Jersey* would be the first to be reactivated, with the first money for the project budgeted in 1981, *Iowa* would be next, with the long lead money budgeted in Fiscal Year 1982.

Unlike the previous recommissionings of the ships, this time extensive work was done. The boilers were converted to burn Diesel Fuel Marine rather than bunker oil, a sewage collection system installed, extensive revisions were made to the electronics suite, and significantly, four of the 5-inch 38-caliber dual-purpose mounts were removed making way for installation of thirty-two long-range Tomahawk cruise missiles in armored box launchers. Also included in the refit were sixteen Harpoon medium-range missiles and four close-in weapons systems (CIWS) to protect the vessel from missile or aircraft attack. Importantly for the crew, air conditioning was added to the vessels.

During the summer of 1982, preliminary work to recommission the *Iowa* was done at the Philadelphia Naval Shipyard. The vessel was then towed to the Avondale shipyard in New Orleans for further work, and then on to Ingalls Shipbuilding in Pascagoula, Mississippi, for completion. *Iowa* was recommissioned on April 28, 1984, ahead of schedule and within budget.

She rejoined the fleet and took part in numerous training exercises as well as calling on various ports in the Atlantic, Mediterranean, and Caribbean to both "show the flag" and provide humanitarian aid. In 1986, she served as President Reagan's reviewing stand for the International Naval Review.

The *Iowa* is seen here docked at the Philadelphia Naval Shipyard in or around August 1982. The following month, the ship would be towed to New Orleans for initial repairs. Scaffolding has been erected at various points alongside the superstructure.

The fleet tug USS *Apache* (T-ATF-172) in the foreground tows the *Iowa* from the Philadelphia Naval Shipyard down the Delaware River on September 1, 1982. This was the first leg of the long trip from Philadelphia to New Orleans. *US Navy*

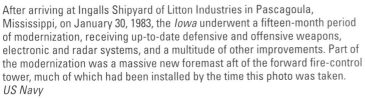

After arriving at Ingalls Shipyard of Litton Industries in Pascagoula, Mississippi, on January 30, 1983, the *Iowa* underwent a fifteen-month period of modernization, receiving up-to-date defensive and offensive weapons, electronic and radar systems, and a multitude of other improvements. Part of the modernization was a massive new foremast aft of the forward fire-control tower, much of which had been installed by the time this photo was taken. *US Navy*

The *Iowa* is viewed from astern during the early part of its modernization at Ingalls Shipyard. The former 40 mm gun tubs over the stern would remain but would be put to other uses. Note the racks for clips of 40 mm ready rounds around the insides of the tubs. Several portable sheds are on the deck to the front of the tubs. *US Navy*

The USS *Norton Sound* (AVM-1) is moored in the foreground adjacent to the *Iowa* at Pascagoula in this aerial view taken on June 17, 1983. Temporary scaffolding is installed around both smokestacks. The *Iowa* was the second of the *Iowa*-class battleships to be modernized, the first being the *New Jersey*. *US Navy*

Almost two months after the preceding photo was taken, modernization continues on the battleship *Iowa* at Pascagoula, Mississippi, on August 19, 1983. Yet to be installed were the electronic countermeasures (ECM), communications, radar, air-defense, and surface-warfare weapons systems that would make *Iowa* a warship fit for modern naval combat. *US Navy*

The *Iowa* is seen from water level at Pascagoula on August 19, 1983. Above the foretop is a tall antenna for TACAN (tactical air navigation system) and radio transmission. Temporary staging platforms and safety rails for workmen have been erected around that antenna. Note the series of portable work platforms arranged along the hull adjacent to the main deck. *US Navy*

The following sequence of color photos of the *Iowa* during her modernization was taken at Ingalls Shipbuilding at Pascagoula, Mississippi, on September 23, 1983. Hundreds of pieces of plywood had been laid down on the deck to protect the wooden decking beneath. The plywood was carefully cut to fit around such things as the breakwater, the barbettes, and deck fittings. *US Navy*

The foredeck and Turrets 1 and 2 are viewed from high up in the superstructure of the *Iowa*. Toward the right front of the roof of Turret 2 is a collapsible tripod. This would be used when the ship became operational for attaching a highline, for transferring materiel from ship to ship. On the left side of the roof of Turret 1 are two beams for use in lowering 16-inch ammunition through hatches in the deck to magazines belowdecks. *US Navy*

Iowa is viewed off her port bow on September 23, 1983. On the forecastle to the lower left is a new feature: a support frame for a Naval Tactical Data System (NTDS) antenna array. This was the US Navy's first system for the automatic collection of tactical information on enemy targets, gathering data from sensors on the ship and other sources and rapidly processing the data. The NTDS monopole antenna would be mounted on the drum-shaped base. *US Navy*

Turrets 1 and 2 are viewed from above, with a portable shed positioned between them. Black bucklers, or bloomers, are mounted on the gun barrels to seal off the gaps betwen them and the frontal plates of the gun houses. The 16-inch gun turrets remained largely unchanged from their original appearances. *US Navy*

The superstructure of the *Iowa* is observed from the forward port quarter. To the left are the top level of the conning tower and the enclosed navigating bridge. Aft of the conning tower is the foundation for the forward Mk.37 secondary-battery director. There would be four such directors, as in the original configuration of the ship. Two new structures, painted green for now, are visible: a two-story compartment abutting the bottom front of the forward fire-control tower, containing a control station and workshop for the Mk.15 Phalanx Close-In Weapons System (CIWS); and a greatly enlarged air-defense level, now containing an electronic-countermeasures compartment, at the top of the forward fire-control tower, just below the forward main-battery director. *US Navy*

A part of the greatly improved offensive punch of the modernized *Iowa*-class battleships was a battery of Tomahawk long-range, all-weather, subsonic cruise missiles. There were eight armored box launchers (ABLs) on the 03 level of the superstructure of the *Iowa*, each of which contained four Tomahawks. At the center of this photo, between the two smokestacks, is a new platform, designed for mounting four of the ABLs. The rest of the ABLs were mounted on a platform near the rear of the superstructure. *US Navy*

In a continuation of the preceding view panning to aft, Turret 3 is seen from above during the *Iowa*'s modernization at Ingalls Shipyard in Pascagoula. On the roof of the turret is equipment for handling UNREP (underway replenishment) highlines, including a collapsible tripod. Jutting from the roof to the front of the right hood for the rangefinder is mounted a boom for lowering 16-inch ammunition through a hatch adjacent to the barbette to magazines far belowdecks. *US Navy*

The rear of the superstructure is seen from above and to the port during September 1983. The aft fire-control tower, also designated the aft main-battery director barbette, is at the upper center. The deck around it, strewn with equipment and building materials, is being prepared as a platform for four Tomahawk ABLs. The round structure aft of the fire-control tower is the foundation of the aft secondary-battery director. *US Navy*

The area from Turret 3 to the stern is viewed from above. The main deck aft of the turret was being prepared as a helipad, to enable helicopters to land on and take off from the battleship. *US Navy*

Iowa is observed off her starboard stern at Ingalls Shipbuilding in September 1983. Scaffolding for workmen is rigged alongside the hull at various points. Scaffolding also is present around the superstructure. Two new features are visible. One is the refueling outrigger for handling fuel lines during underway replenishment (UNREP) operation, also called the replenishment at sea (RAS) king post, to the starboard side of the aft fire-control tower. The other feature is the large, arch-shaped boat davit located on the main deck between the smokestacks. *US Navy*

Even in the age of guided missiles and high-speed aircraft and water craft, the venerable 5-inch/38-caliber dual-purpose gun still had a place in the US Navy. A refurbished twin 5-inch/38-caliber gun mount is being prepared for mounting on the *Iowa* in September 1983. The armored gun house is being lowered onto the mount, and subsequently the two 5-inch/38-caliber dual-purpose guns will be mounted. *US Navy*

After Ingalls Shipbuilding completed work on the *Iowa*, the battleship was subjected to sea trials in the Gulf of Mexico to test its systems and identify any problems so that they could be remedied before the ship was recommissioned. In this March 9, 1984, photo of the guns of Turret 1 being test-fired, a 16-inch projectile is visible in flight to the left. The ship's 16-inch/50-caliber Mk.7 guns had a muzzle velocity of about 2,500 feet per second when firing armor-piercing projectiles.

Iowa test fires the 16-inch/50-caliber Mk.7 guns of Turret 1 at high elevation to port during trials in April 1984. The decks have been cleared of personnel, but many people may be seen on the navigating bridge and on other levels of the superstructure, observing the display of the ship's firepower. *US Navy*

On April 5, 1984, just over three weeks before her April 28, 1984 recommissioning, the *Iowa* undergoes her first high-speed sea trials following her modernization. This was the first time the ship had proceeded at speed under her own power since 1958. The ship's number, 61, was painted in large numerals on the bow in white with black shadowing. *US Navy*

Members of the battleship *Iowa*'s recommissioning crew, including officers, sailors, and crewmen, salute for the viewers of the TV show *Good Morning America* during a dress rehearsal for the ship's April 28, 1984, recommissioning ceremony. Most of the men visible here are standing on the roofs of Turrets 1 and 2 on the first level of the superstructure. Footrails are present along the edges of the turret roofs. *US Navy*

Modernization and sea trials of USS *Iowa* completed, the battleship is dressed fore and aft with flags and decorated with bunting in preparation for the battleship's recommissioning ceremony at Ingalls Shipbuilding Division of Litton Industries, at Pascagoula, Mississippi, on April 28, 1984. This ceremony marked the formal reactivation of the battleship in the US Navy. Actually, it was the *Iowa*'s second recommissioning, the first having occurred on August 25, 1951. To the right are bleachers and seating for some of the attendees. *US Navy*

Against a backdrop of the two forward twin 5-inch/38-caliber gun mounts of the port side of USS *Iowa*, Vice President George H.W. Bush addresses the dignitaries, crew, and invited guests at the April 28, 1984, recommissioning. In his address, Bush said, "This is truly a beautiful ship," and he quipped that he felt like a father "giving away a bride at the wedding." *US Navy*

Capt. Gerald E. Gneckow, lower left, commanding officer of USS *Iowa*, speaks at the ship's recommissioning on April 28, 1984. Among the dignitaries attending the ceremony are Vice President George H.W. Bush, center, holding the portfolio, and Secretary of the Navy John Lehman. *US Navy*

Officers of the USS *Iowa* run along the dock and up the gangway at the ship's commissioning ceremony. The *Iowa*'s bunting-decorated forecastle is visible to the upper right. *US Navy*

USS *Iowa* is anchored in Guantánamo Bay, Cuba, on May 18, 1984. After her recommissioning, the battleship spent two weeks at Guantánamo while her crew underwent refresher training. Note the three boats moored to the boat boom toward the stern. The refueling outrigger is noticeable to the side of the rear of the superstructure. *US Navy*

Following her training visit to Guantánamo Bay, the *Iowa* steamed to waters off Vieques Island, Puerto Rico, which served as a US Navy target range. In this dramatic aerial photograph, the 16-inch/50-caliber guns of the *Iowa* fire a full broadside during a training exercise on July 1, 1984, creating circular shock waves on the water. Note the helipad on the aft part of the main deck. *Naval History and Heritage Command*

In an aerial view off the port bow, the 16-inch/50-caliber guns of turret 2 unleash a volley to starboard. Both of the Mk.38 main-battery directors are trained to starboard in order to provide control for the three 16-inch gun turrets. *US Navy*

In March 1985, off the Naval Weapons Station at Yorktown, Virginia, 16-inch projectiles are being prepared for offloading from the foredeck of USS *Iowa*. Discussing the operation are, left to right, Weapons Officer Cmdr. Richard Gano, Executive Officer Capt. John J. Chernesky, and Commanding Officer Capt. Gerald E. Gneckow. In the background is the support frame and base for the NTDS antenna. The ammunition was being offloaded in preparation for the ship's going into dry dock. *US Navy*

Iowa's 16-inch/50-caliber guns fire a broadside to port in nearly nighttime conditions. On the side of the superstructure is the white shape of the radome of one of the Mk.15 Phalanx CIWS defensive guns. Note the sharp inward curve in the line of the deck from abeam Turret 1 to the forecastle. *US Navy*

In May 1985, USS *Iowa* is in Dry Dock Number 4 at the Norfolk Naval Shipyard, Portsmouth, Virginia, for repairs and maintenance on her hull. The ship entered the dry dock on April 26, and remained there until July 31. Massive keel blocks, upon which ships' hulls rest while in the dry dock, are lined up on both sides of the dry dock. *US Navy*

USS *Iowa* is viewed from the rear in Dry Dock Number 4 at the Norfolk Naval Shipyard in May 1985. The battleship was undergoing four months of post-shakedown availability (PSA) repairs to remedy mechanical and structural problems discovered during the ship's shakedown following her recommissioning. *US Navy*

Technicians in Dry Dock 4 at Norfolk Naval Shipyard provide a sense of scale to one of the two inboard propellers of USS *Iowa*. The inboard propellers had five blades while the outboard propellers had four. The skeg to the front of the propeller also is visible. *US Navy*

The guided-missile frigate USS *Halyburton* (FFG-40) is taking on fuel from USS *Iowa* during Exercise Ocean Safari in September 1985. This was a naval exercise to gauge NATO's ability to keep the cross-Atlantic sea lanes open in the event of a war with the Soviet Union. A fuel line is faintly visible from aft of the *Halyburton*'s mainmast to the refueling outrigger on the *Iowa*. *US Navy*

On October 17, 1985, USS *Iowa* fires a broadside of its 16-inch/50-caliber guns during Operation BALTOPS, an annual training exercise in the Baltic Sea conducted by the Commander, United States Naval Forces Europe. The 1985 BALTOPS had a political subtext: to impress on the Soviets the NATO navies' right to operate in international waters near the Soviet coasts. *US Navy*

In an aerial view related to the top left image, *Halyburton* and *Iowa* move in close formation as the guided-missile frigate takes on fuel from the *Iowa*. Capital ships, with their large capacities for fuel, often were tasked with refueling smaller ships during ocean passages. *US Navy*

USS *Iowa* and USS *Halyburton* are viewed from a slightly different angle during the refueling operation. Note the large US flag painted on the roof of *Iowa*'s Turret 1. A corridor along the route of the anchor chains on the foredeck, from the wildcats to the hawse holes, was painted a dark color. The wooden decks were unpainted. *US Navy*

Crewmen of the USS *Iowa* in dress whites man the rails as the battleship departs from Fort Lauderdale, Florida, on February 18, 1986. The *Iowa* was en route to Central America. Note the white awning over the bridge in front of the primary conning station midway up the forward fire-control tower. *US Navy*

The *Iowa* is moored at one of the Brooklyn piers in May 1986, during a visit to New York City. The ship is dressed fore and aft with flags. Although the two 20 mm antiaircraft guns on the forecastle had been removed decades earlier, the platform and splinter shield for them remained on the forecastle. *US Navy*

On February 24, 1986, USS *Iowa* passes through the Pedro Miguel Locks of the Panama Canal. The battleship was in the region as part of a US move to show its support for friendly governments in Central America and express its interest in the region. *US Navy*

On the same occasion as in the top right photo, the *Iowa* is viewed from the rear, with some of the skyscrapers of lower Manhattan looming in the right background. Below the name "IOWA" on the stern are two fittings installed during the ship's modernization. These are doors for the AN/SLQ-25 Nixie torpedo countermeasures devices: towed decoys that emit signals simulating the ship's engine and propeller sounds in order to divert a torpedo from its selected target. *US Navy*

In a view of USS *Iowa* at an unidentified harbor in mid-1986, a number of colorful markings are on the bulwark of the navigating bridge. Most of the markings are symbols for various excellence or efficiency awards. To the right is a display of campaign ribbons pertaining to the *Iowa*'s operations over the decades. A white "E" efficiency award is also on the forward Mk.37 secondary-battery director. *US Navy*

As seen from the foredeck of USS *Iowa*, a BGM-109 Tomahawk cruise missile has just been test-fired on August 2, 1986, at the Eglin Air Force Base range in the Gulf of Mexico. The Tomahawk was produced in numerous variants. The BGM-109A was a land-attack nuclear missile that remained in service until around 2013, while the BGM-109C was a conventional land-attack missile and the BGM-109D was a cluster-munitions dispenser missile for land attack. *US Navy*

The top of *Iowa*'s aft smokestack is viewed from the starboard side in this mid-1986 photo. To the front of the smokestack cap is a protective dome for a communications antenna for the RQ-2 Pioneer unmanned aerial vehicle (UAV), a gunnery-spotting and reconnaissance drone introduced in 1986. The RQ-2 communications antenna and dome first made their appearance on the *Iowa* in August 1986. To the lower left is the Mk.13 radar antenna mounted above the aft Mk.38 director. *US Navy*

The 16-inch/50-caliber Mk.7 guns of USS *Iowa* fire a broadside during gunnery practice off Colón, Panama, on January 27, 1987. During that month, the *Iowa* participated in the training exercise BLASTEX 1-87 in the Caribbean and visited ports in Honduras, Colombia, and the Virgin Islands. *US Navy*

The following series of photographs, taken in December 1986, documents how 16-inch ammunition was transferred from the storage areas below the turrets up to the 16-inch /50-caliber guns. Here, 16-inch projectiles (olive-drab for live rounds and blue for practice rounds) are stored on their bases in a projectile flat several levels below the gun house floor. To the right of center is a projectile hoist, which, along with the ring-shaped section of floor beneath it, traversed in unison with the guns. *US Navy*

Projectiles were moved from their storage places on the projectile flat by means of a procedure called parbuckling, whereby a motorized "gypsy head" capstan (center) operated a line routed around a pulley and the lower part of the projectile. In the case shown here, the projectile is being skidded from its storage spot on the outer ring to the inner ring, which rotated in either direction so as to bring the projectile as close as possible to a projectile hoist. There were six gypsy heads on each projectile flat. Projectiles were secured by large roller chains known as projectile lashings. *US Navy*

The projectile has now been slid onto the center ring of the projectile flat by means of a parbuckling gear. The outer ring of the projectile flat, where the blue practice shells in the background are stored, was fixed and did not rotate. All three concentric rings of the projectile-flat floor are visible at the bottom of the photo, and the surfaces were of unpainted steel. *US Navy*

The nose of a 16-inch practice shell is coming into view in a projectile hoist leading up to one of USS *Iowa*'s turrets. Each 16-inch gun was served by one projectile hoist, and these featured a two-way rack and pawl powered by an electro-hydraulic drive. *US Navy*

The 1,000th 16-inch projectile to be fired by USS *Iowa* since the ship's 1984 recommissioning has just come up to the top of one of the projectile hoists in Turret Number 2 and is poised in the loading cradle. In the next step, the projectile will be brought into line with the spanning tray to the front of the projectile fuse and then rammed into the gun chamber. Standing on a platform to the right rear of the breech of the 16-inch gun is the gun captain, who has on his left arm a long, thick glove for wiping the gas-check pad when the breech was opened. *US Navy*

Three 16-inch bagged propellant charges at a time were delivered by hoist to the locker at the top of the photo, the door of which would mechanically swing down so the charges could roll down the door to the spanning tray to the rear of the gun breech. The gun captain, right, and two crewmen are arranging the bags on the spanning tray prior to ramming the charges into the chamber. Six such bags were necessary to fire a 16-inch projectile.

The gun captain is pointing to the door of the powder hoist to indicate that he is ready for three more bagged propellant charges. The red patches with quilted designs on the rears of the bags contained detonating powder. At the top of the photo is the closed, piston-operated door of the powder hoist. *US Navy*

During a firing of the 16-inch/50-caliber gun in the USS *Iowa*, the barrel has recoiled; notice the position of the rear of the breech with reference to the powder-hoist door compared with the preceding photo. Two counter-recoil cylinders are above the breech; grooves are incorporated into the top of the yoke to provide clearance for the cylinders. *US Navy*

The left guns of Turrets 1, 2, and 3 of USS *Iowa* have just fired a broadside to starboard during a NATO training exercise in December 1988; a stream of smoke is issuing from each of those 16-inch/50-caliber gun barrels. Visible on the after part of the main deck are the highly visible white lines and circle that served as visual aids for helicopter pilots landing on the helipad. *US Navy*

A CH-53E Super Stallion helicopter is hovering over the helipad on the USS *Iowa* during a 1987 cruise. In the foreground the guns of Turret 3 are traversed to about the two o'clock position. Even nearer in the foreground and partially hidden by the corner post of the handrails is the stabilized glide-slope indicator assembly, part of a system for transmitting glide-slope data to helicopter pilots to facilitate landings on the helipad. *US Navy*

The port side of the bridge area of USS *Iowa* is the focus of this photograph taken at Naval Station, Norfolk, Virginia, October 1988. Efficiency and excellence awards and campaign ribbons are marked on the side of the navigating bridge. Above the center of the photo is one of the Mk.15 Phalanx close-in weapons systems (CIWS) mounts, featuring a white radome and a 20 mm Gatling gun. The CIWS relied on the ship's radars to automatically identify threats to the ship and fire on them. *US Navy*

At 0955 on the morning of April 19, 1989, an explosion tore through the center gun room of Turret 2. The blast killed forty-seven sailors manning the massive guns. Initially, the Navy suggested that this may have been the result of sabotage on the part of one of the gun crew, but they later retreated from that position. *US Navy*

Tung Thanh Adams	Fire Controlman 3rd class (FC3)	Alexandria, VA
Robert Wallace Backherms	Gunner's Mate 3rd class (GM3)	Ravenna, OH
Dwayne Collier Battle	Electrician's Mate, Fireman Apprentice (EMFA)	Rocky Mount, NC
Walter Scot Blakey	Gunner's Mate 3rd class (GM3)	Eaton Rapids, MI
Pete Edward Bopp	Gunner's Mate 3rd class (GM3)	Levittown, NY
Ramon Jarel Bradshaw	Seaman Recruit (SR)	Tampa, FL
Philip Edward Buch	Lieutenant, Junior Grade (LTjg)	Las Cruces, NM
Eric Ellis Casey	Seaman Apprentice (SA)	Mt. Airy, NC
John Peter Cramer	Gunners Mate 2nd class (GM2)	Uniontown, PA
Milton Francis Devaul Jr.	Gunners Mate 3rd class (GM3)	Solvay, NY
Leslie Allen Everhart Jr.	Seaman Apprentice (SA)	Cary, NC
Gary John Fisk	Boatswains Mate 2nd class (BM2)	Oneida, NY
Tyrone Dwayne Foley	Seaman (SN)	Bullard, TX
Robert James Gedeon III	Seaman Apprentice (SA)	Lakewood, OH
Brian Wayne Gendron	Seaman Apprentice (SA)	Madera, CA
John Leonard Goins	Seaman Recruit (SR)	Columbus, OH
David L. Hanson	Electricians Mate 3rd class (EM3)	Perkins, SD
Ernest Edward Hanyecz	Gunners Mate 1st class (GM1)	Bordentown, NJ
Clayton Michael Hartwig	Gunners Mate 2nd class (GM2)	Cleveland, OH
Michael William Helton	Legalman 1st class (LN1)	Louisville, KY
Scott Alan Holt	Seaman Apprentice (SA)	Fort Meyers, FL
Reginald L. Johnson Jr.	Seaman Recruit (SR)	Warrensville Heights, OH
Nathaniel Clifford Jones Jr.	Seaman Apprentice (SA)	Buffalo, NY
Brian Robert Jones	Seaman (SN)	Kennesaw, GA
Michael Shannon Justice	Seaman (SN)	Matewan, WV
Edward J. Kimble	Seaman (SN)	Ft. Stockton, TX
Richard E. Lawrence	Gunners Mate 3rd class (GM3)	Springfield, OH
Richard John Lewis	Fire Controlman, Seaman Apprentice (FCSA)	Northville, MI
Jose Luis Martinez Jr.	Seaman Apprentice (SA)	Hidalgo, TX
Todd Christopher McMullen	Boatswains Mate 3rd class (BM3)	Manheim, PA
Todd Edward Miller	Seaman Recruit (SR)	Ligonier, PA
Robert Kenneth Morrison	Legalman 1st class (LN1)	Jacksonville, FL
Otis Levance Moses	Seaman (SN)	Bridgeport, CN
Darin Andrew Ogden	Gunners Mate 3rd class (GM3)	Shelbyville, IN
Ricky Ronald Peterson	Seaman (SN)	Houston, MN
Mathew Ray Price	Gunners Mate 3rd class (GM3)	Burnside, PA
Harold Earl Romine Jr.	Seaman Recruit (SR)	Brandenton, FL
Geoffrey Scott Schelin	Gunners Mate 3rd class (GMG3)	Costa Mesa, CA
Heath Eugene Stillwagon	Gunners Mate 3rd class (GM3)	Connellsville, PA
Todd Thomas Tatham	Seaman Recruit (SR)	Wolcott, NY
Jack Ernest Thompson	Gunners Mate 3rd class (GM3)	Greeneville, TN
Stephen J. Welden	Gunners Mate 2nd class (GM2)	Yukon, OK
James Darrell White	Gunners Mate 3rd class (GM3)	Norwalk, CA
Rodney Maurice White	Seaman Recruit (SR)	Louisville, KY
Michael Robert Williams	Boatswains Mate 2nd class (BM2)	South Shore, KY
John Rodney Young	Seaman (SN)	Rockhill, SC
Reginald Owen Ziegler	Senior Chief Gunners Mate (GMCS)	Port Gibson, NY

The fireball brought about by the explosion of Turret 2's center gun room threatened to ignite the below-decks powder magazine, detonation of which would have certainly sunk *Iowa* with a tremendous loss of life. Fortunately, the decades-old safety features built into the turret complex worked as designed, which combined with the quick flooding of the magazines prevented an even greater tragedy. *US Navy*

Damage control teams spray tons of water onto and into the damaged Turret 2. The heat from the fires inside could be felt in the decks below. Firefighting activities lasted for several hours after the initial explosion. *US Navy*

At 0955 on April 19, 1989, while conducting operations off of Puerto Rico, there was an explosion in the center gun room of turret 2. These operations were observed by VADM Jerome Johnson and his staff from the bridge. The firing exercises began at 0933 with turret 1's left gun, which misfired. The turret crew was unable to make the giant cannon fire. Counter to peacetime protocols, which required the turret 1 fault be cleared before resuming main battery fire, Capt. Fred Moosally, *Iowa*'s commander, ordered turret 2 to load and fire a salvo.

Forty-four seconds later Lt. Phil Buch, the turret 2 officer, reported that turret 2's right gun was ready to fire, and seventeen seconds later the left gun was reported in the same condition. Moments later, it was reported from the center gun room that there was a problem in that room. Interphone traffic recorded center gun captain Richard Errick Lawrence announcing, "I'm not ready yet! I'm not ready yet!" This was followed by turret 2's leading petty officer Ernie Hanyecz saying, "Mort! Mort! Mort!" Next is heard Senior Chief Reggie Ziegler shouting, "Oh, my God! The power is smoldering!" Finally, petty officer Hanyecz can be heard yelling, "Oh, my God! There's a flash!"

Turret 2's center gun exploded, sending a fireball over 2,500 degrees sweeping through the turret at 2,000 feet per second. While blast doors protected the men in the magazine spaces beneath the turret, and quickly flooding turret 2's magazine area prevented the ensuing fire from detonating the tons of powder stored there, the forty-seven men in *Iowa*'s turret were killed instantly.

The bodies of the forty-seven *Iowa* sailors killed in the blast were flown to Roosevelt Roads Naval Station, and then to the Center for Mortuary Affairs at Dover Air Force Base, Delaware, where this photograph was taken. It was later revealed that seven men died from blast injuries and ten from blunt force injuries. Several men were found to be wearing gas masks in a futile attempt to protect themselves from the poisonous gases given off by the burning wear-reducing jackets wrapping the powder bags, indicating they may have survived the initial blast, only to succumb to the ensuing fire. *US Navy*

Commander J.P. Morse, commanding officer of USS *Iowa*, signs the final entry in the battleship's logbook as the warship is decommissioned for the last time. The ceremony was held inside due to rain. *US Navy*

Several months after the *Iowa*'s final decommissioning, workers are adjusting the mooring lines of the ship at the Philadelphia Naval Shipyard on June 26, 1991. As part of the ship's deactivation, many of the antennas and small components had been removed from the ship, but the Naval Tactical Data System (NTDS) antenna array remained in place on its mount above the forecastle.

As a result of the government's closing of the Philadelphia Naval Shipyard, the decommissioned battleship *Iowa* was relocated to the Naval Education and Training Center in Rhode Island. In this September 24, 1998, photograph, the ship is under tow and has just passed beneath the Claiborne Pell Newport Bridge en route to the Center. *US Navy*

Sister battleships *Iowa* and, partially visible next to her, *Wisconsin*, decommissioned on September 30, 1991, are moored side by side at the Philadelphia Naval Shipyard on September 9, 1993. Both ships still retained their massive, black mainmasts. Tomahawk armored box launchers were still present on the *Iowa*. *US Navy*

From March 8, to April 21, 2001, the battleship *Iowa* began the long journey under tow to Suisun Bay, California, where the ship would be berthed for the next decade. From 2001 to 2006, she was assigned to the Pacific Reserve Fleet. In this close-up of a NASA photograph taken in or around 2011, the *Iowa* is on the right side of a long row of decommissioned naval ships. *NASA*

CHAPTER 9
Preservation

This view of the *Iowa* from her forecastle was taken shortly after the *Iowa* docked at Richmond, California, in late October 2011, where she would undergo an extensive restoration. This perspective offers a good view of the NTDS antenna as well as the method of securing the anchor chains with stoppers: short safety chains bolted to the deck and attached to the anchor chains with pelican hooks to relieve the strain on the chains imposed by the massive weight of the anchors. *Chris Hughes*

Although not completely repaired following the turret 2 explosion, *Iowa* returned to fleet operations in June 1989, steaming to Europe and the Mediterranean. Returning to Norfolk in November, during the transatlantic crossing *Iowa* fired her 16-inch guns for the last time. She had fired 2,873 16-inch rounds since recommissioning in 1984, and 11,834 since her launch.

She arrived in Norfolk on December 7, 1989, and remained there tied up until decommissioned for the last time on October 26, 1990. First laid up again in Philadelphia, as a result of that yard's closure she was towed to the Naval Education and Training Center in Newport, Rhode Island, where she remained until March 8, 2001. During this time she was struck from the Navy list in 1995. In 1999, the Strom Thurmond National Defense Authorization Act required that the *Iowa* and *Wisconsin* be returned to the Navy list. This was done to pave the way for donation of the *New Jersey*, which had been maintained in reserve, for use as a memorial. In 2001, *Iowa was* towed to Suisun Bay, near San Francisco, joining the reserve fleet there, in accordance with the 1999 provisions. In 2006, the Secretary of the Navy again struck *Iowa* from the Navy list, and shortly thereafter Congress mandated that the *Iowa* and *Wisconsin* be kept and maintained in a state of readiness and able to be returned to service. In May 2010, the Navy made the *Iowa* available for donation as a memorial. After an abortive attempt to berth the ship at the former Mare Island Naval Shipyard, and failed efforts by Stockton and San Francisco, a group in San Pedro rallied as the Pacific Battleship Center. Unlike the other efforts, this group secured the site and financing required by the Navy to ensure the preservation of this historic warship.

The *Iowa*'s Turret 2 and her superstructure are viewed from the front at Richmond, California. The ship underwent rehabilitation there starting in October 2011, to prepare her for being placed on permanent display as a museum ship at the Pacific Battleship Center at the Port of Los Angeles, California. Mounted above the forward Mk.37 secondary-battery director is a dish-type Mk.25 radar antenna. *Chris Hughes*

As viewed from off the amidship starboard beam while the *Iowa* was docked at Richmond, to the lower left is the starboard boat davit. At the center is the starboard Mk.37 secondary-battery director and its Mk.25 radar antenna. Rising above are the forward smokestack, the main support structure of the mainmast, and the superstructure. *Chris Hughes*

The superstructure of the *Iowa* is seen from the starboard side at Richmond before restoration of the ship got underway. Essentially it was still in the same condition as when it was mothballed at Suisun Bay. On the railing along the main deck is a banner with a subtle pitch for sponsors for the restoration along with the organization's website address. *Chris Hughes*

The aft smokestack and a twin 5-inch/38-caliber dual-purpose gun mount are viewed from the starboard side. On the side of the smokestack is a remnant from the ship's past active service: an "E" efficiency award in red with black shadowing, representing that the award was for engineering or survivability. *Chris Hughes*

The *Iowa* is seen from the port side of the quarterdeck while docked at Richmond, California. Instead of flexible bucklers, rigid covers had been fitted over the juncture between the 16-inch gun barrels and the frontal armor of the gun house, to seal out the elements while the ship was in long-term storage. Above the turret is the upper part of the replenishment at sea (RAS) king post. The radar antenna had been removed from the Mk.38 main-battery director. *Chris Hughes*

In a view from the starboard side of the *Iowa* at Richmond around 2011, the structure with the railing on top to the immediate front of the aft smokestack is a two-story deck house that, during its 1990s configuration, housed an ordnance workshop and a close-in weapons systems (CIWS) workshop. *Chris Hughes*

Chained to the metal deck of the helipad of the *Iowa* in this view facing forward from the wooden-decked fantail is the foretop platform, which will be reinstalled during the ship's restoration. Lying by the side of the platform are sections of railings and other structural components. Visible in the distance is the foremast. *Chris Hughes*

Structures of the aft portion of the superstructure of the *Iowa* are viewed from the starboard side, from the rearward-tilting helicopter control booth to the left, above the rear of Turret 3, to the aft smokestack to the right. At the center above its conical foundation is the aft Mk.38 main-battery director. Also in view is the RAS king post. *Chris Hughes*

The forecastle of the *Iowa* is viewed from a spot on the starboard side of the main deck aft of the wildcats. With some of the wooden deck planks having been taken up, the severely corroded and scaling condition of the steel deck below the planking is obvious. *Chris Hughes*

The superstructure of the *Iowa* is observed from the forward port quarter with scaffolding in place while undergoing restoration at Richmond. The panels that had been installed over the windows of the navigating bridge when the ship was decommissioned were still in place at this time. *Chris Hughes*

Restoration of the *Iowa* is well underway at Richmond, California, with extensive scaffolding erected around the superstructure and smokestacks. This was still relatively early in the restoration work, before the ship was repainted and major and minor exterior components that had been removed were reinstalled. *Chris Hughes*

Containment netting has been rigged to the rear of the forward part of the superstructure and the starboard Harpoon anti-ship missile launchers abeam the forward smokestack. Between the 5-inch gun mounts toward the right is the starboard boat davit, while to the left of center is the RAS king post. *Chris Hughes*

In late May 2012, the fully restored battleship *Iowa* was towed from Richmond, California, to the Port of Los Angeles, where she now is the centerpiece of the Pacific Warship Museum. In the first of a series of photos of the *Iowa* in August 2016, Turrets 1 and 2 and the front of the superstructure are viewed from the forward part of the main deck. In the foreground are the hand wheels for braking the anchor chain, along with a hatch and two ventilators.

The forecastle is in the background of this view over the tops of Turrets 1 and 2. Two periscope heads and their covers are toward the rear of the roof of Turret 1.

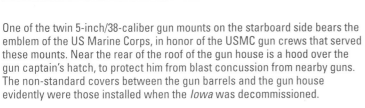

One of the twin 5-inch/38-caliber gun mounts on the starboard side bears the emblem of the US Marine Corps, in honor of the USMC gun crews that served these mounts. Near the rear of the roof of the gun house is a hood over the gun captain's hatch, to protect him from blast concussion from nearby guns. The non-standard covers between the gun barrels and the gun house evidently were those installed when the *Iowa* was decommissioned.

Behind the handrails and netting in the lower foreground are Mk.36 SRBOC launchers, for firing chaff cartridges to interfere with the electronics of enemy anti-ship missiles. Above the SRBOC launchers is the starboard Mk.37 secondary-battery director, above which are the foremast and its radar platform and the forward fire-control tower.

In a view from the starboard side of the quarterdeck of *Iowa* facing forward in August 2016, structures include the left side of Turret 3 in the left foreground, the RAS king post in the right foreground, the aft main-battery and secondary-battery directors, the aft starboard Tomahawk armored-box launcher, the aft smokestack, and the foremast. Above the foretop are the tall TACAN/radio-transmitter antenna and the SPS-49 air-search radar antenna.

One of the starboard Tomahawk missile armored-box launchers (ABLs) is viewed from the left front with its access doors open. On the inside are launching racks for four BGM-109 Tomahawk Cruise Missiles. On the inside of the right door are schematic diagrams for the ABL.

This is the interior of the *Iowa*'s "new" combat information center (CIC), where constantly updated information on enemy threats in the air, on the surface, and below the water was collected and plotted, to provide the most comprehensive picture of the battle space possible.

The roof and the 16-inch/50-caliber guns of Turret Number 3 and the helipad are viewed from the platform to the rear of the foundation of the aft Mk.37 secondary-battery director. In the foreground are two spotlights, part of an array of spotlights positioned above the helicopter control booth. On the turret roof is a collapsible tripod for attaching a highline for ship-to-ship transfers of men and materials.

The two main-battery plot rooms were where data from the Mk.38 main-battery directors was collected and processed to calculate firing solutions for the 16-inch/50-caliber guns. This is the forward main-battery plot. In the foreground is the top of the Mk.41 Stable Vertical, a gyroscope-based instrument that calculated the ship's roll and pitch with reference to the Mk.38 director's line of sight and the ship's course and speed.

The face of one of the *Iowa*'s boilers is depicted. There are eight boilers, with two in each of the four fire rooms. Manufactured by Babcock & Wilcox, they are of three-drum, double-furnace design. The boilers furnished steam to four geared-turbine units to provide propulsion for the ship.

From the rear of each of the turbine assemblies, a propeller shaft proceeds aft to its respective propeller. Shown here is the propeller shaft to the rear of Turbine Number 2, the shaft's white housing decorated with red and blue tape.

Shown here is *Iowa*'s Turbine Number 2. The *Iowa* has four turbine assemblies: one for each propeller. These assemblies consist of a high-pressure turbine, a low-pressure turbine, and a double-reduction gear.

Throughout the battleship *Iowa*, there is an extensive amount of crew art, commemorative stencilings and inscriptions preserved on bulkheads, fixtures, and other surfaces. An example is this list of the members of the decommissioning crew in Engine Room Number 2: that is, the personnel at the time of the ship's third and final decommissioning on October 26, 1990.

In a view from the fantail forward in August 2016, the deckhouse on the near side of Turret 3 is the *Iowa*'s aviation service center. On the rear of the roof are three signal lights, each of which is under a hood. Mounted on the roof of the aviation service center is a whip antenna complete with truss cables.

The starboard side of the fantail of the *Iowa* is depicted. The former gun tubs for the stern quad 40 mm gun mounts were converted in the 1980s to other purposes. The starboard tub, seen here, was used for stowing lines, helicopter starting cables, and other gear, while the port tub now served as a helicopter fueling station. Also in view are the flag staff, the stern chocks, and to the immediate port side of the flag staff, the stern-lights assembly.

Today *Iowa* is preserved as a memorial and museum in San Pedro, California, keeping alive the memory not only of her many crews, but all battleship sailors, and as a powerful reminder of the nation's sea power. *US Navy*